HECTOR AND ACHILLES

EDWARD EATON

A Verse Drama Published by
Dragonfly Publishing, Inc.

Hector and Achilles
A Verse Drama

Paperback Edition
EAN 978-1-936381-63-0
ISBN 1-936381-63-X]

Published in the United States of America by
Dragonfly Publishing, Inc.
Website: www.dragonflypubs.com

TABLE OF CONTENTS

INTERMISSION

As always, I would like to dedicate my work to my wife, Silviya, and my son, Christopher.

Sine quibus non

Dramatis Personae

TROJANS:

Priam	A King	(M) 40s-60s
Hector	His son, Chief General of the Trojans	(M) mid-20s-30s
Andromache	Hector's wife	(F) early 20s
Astynax	Their son; could be played by a woman	(M) 8-10
Briseis	Hector's cousin, Achilles' slave	(F) 15-20

CHORUS OF TROJAN WOMEN:

Trojan Women (1-4 of them)	(F) 20s-30s

GREEKS:

Odysseus	A Greek King	(M) 25-35
Ajax	Another Greek King	(M) 25-35
Achilles	A Greek Hero and General	(M) 20s
Patroclus	Achilles' friend, mentor, and lover	(M) 30-40
Thersites	A hideous Greek soldier	(M) 20-30

CHORUS OF GREEK SOLDIERS:

Greek Soldiers (1-4 of them)	(M) 20s

SETTING:

The following areas are represented on the stage: the Battlefield, the Outskirts of the Greek Camp, the Walls of Troy, and Achilles' Tent.

During part of the play, several locations are used at the same time. There should be no lag or delay between the actions in various locations.

SCENE 1
The Battlefield

Night

The lights come up on two men in an embrace; they stand there—still, but swaying

There is some light from the moon and the stars and from offstage fires—some from campfires, some from fires set by Trojan soldiers

Offstage, the Greek soldiers can be heard fleeing, scared and confused

One of the men, HECTOR, breathes heavily and shudders and sighs

He pulls his sword out of the body of PATROCLUS, who is wearing the armor of ACHILLES

The body of PATROCLUS falls to the ground

Out of breath and sated, HECTOR looks around to make sure he is alone

He prods the body and determines that it is indeed dead

He sighs

HECTOR

Whence comes tonight's light?
Does it come from moon and stars
Or flaming Greek tents?

I think from the camp
That burns so hot and roars to
Mask the screams of death,

But how can that be?
The stars are themselves gods that
Flame in the heavens—

Or so priests tell me.
An inferno lives in each
Tiny prick of light.

A distant god in
Each distant star lives and there
Sees us live our lives.

Are these gods merely
Small and insubstantial points
Just beyond our reach?

Could we leap and grab
These small gods, squeeze and crush them
In our mortal grips?

If they live near man's
Grand and bright cities then they
Are weakened, frailed gods.

I can reach my hands
To these flickering gods and
Feel no divine warmth.

The small campfires that
Warm my enemies and foes
Alike give more heat

And give more light to
Illuminate a page or
The thoughts of tired men.

Weak and distant stars
Can have little to do with
The affairs of men.

Why do we make oaths
And wars in the names of far
Away pricks of light

Or lazy fireflies
That hover impotently
Just out of our reach?

Was it these gods who
Helped me send this puny man
To hell? Did they guide

My sword to his gut?
Did they make me duck faster?
Is my victory

Skill or fate or worse?
Was it the cowardice of
This man's erstwhile friends

Who fled when I came
Alone to this place, my men
Firing the Greek camps?

Man-made fires so hot
We cannot see nor feel far
Away divine flames.

Perhaps these fires and
Not the gods will chase the Greeks
From my city's shores

On which they've lived and
Killed and stolen so many
Years of pointless war.

Years of pointless war.
Why do we fight? Is it for
Paris' sacred love

Decreed by a far
Away Aphrodite, a
Flickering goddess?

Let me have one puff
Of air to extinguish this
Murd'rous divine tramp

Who sends her harlots
To befuddle a foolish
Boy's pride and reason.

This barbarian
Is just an excuse for these
Roughnecks to slaughter

The men and women
Of this great city of Troy
In lust and fury.

Is this gods' justice
Because Menelaus can't
Satisfy his wife?

Or is't man's envy
For Iliums' grandeur and
Great wealth and power?

Has Troy grown so big
This city of light and hope
And jewels must fall

To these bickering
Cowardly hordes of madmen?
Or can we survive?

I look on my Troy
And see the greatness that man
Is capable of.

I look on this camp
And see whence we came. Were my
Ancestors like them?

Hirsute and ill read?
They believe in their gods, gods
Of flame, smoke, and air

Gods snuffed out by the
Weakest gust of winter cold,
The smallest rainstorm.

Troy is forever;
A great island city set
On by hostile seas

That roar and crash 'gainst
Our ancient constant walls and
Slowly wear them down.

Is Troy's light to be
Doused by a final great wave
That wastes her people

Or shall we be mined
By jealousy and collapse
Under our own weight?

This foreign horde stays,
Brought here by foreign storm winds
Bearing foreign gods

And we must change our
Ways, become like them, liking
Them, like ourselves less.

Our great city has
Become a vast cave o'ergrown
By a wilderness.

Perhaps our great light
Will someday be a weakling
Flicker like the stars

Perhaps someday their
Fizzling spark will burst into
Flame engulfing all.

Perhaps we will be
Gods then, and we can watch them
From our distant stars.

SCENE 2
The Outskirts of the Greek Camp
About the same time

THERSITES sits alone, all but unseen

The camp is a mess; broken spears and garbage are strewn all about; whatever the Greeks use for toilets is next to the piles of rotting food

There are small campfires here and there

ODYSSEUS, AJAX, and the CHORUS OF SOLDIERS enter severally; they are running and out of breath

ODYSSEUS

A spear!

AJAX

No! Water!
I am out of breath!

ODYSSEUS

A spear!
I say a spear. Now!

AJAX

Water, then cover.
What good will be a spear when
All Troy's armies come?

I hear them behind
Us. Hide fast and let them pass,
Then we will be safe.

CHORUS OF SOLDIERS

Go sound the alarm.
Raise our allies from their sleep
P'raps they can save us.

ODYSSEUS

Duck or be seen and
Killed by a lucky arrow
Or face a hero—

AJAX

Who will hack at you
And remove your foolish head

ODYSSEUS

Do you call me fool?

CHORUS OF SOLDIERS

Hush, Odysseus.
Put out that fire! How can we
See without the fire?

Call Agamemnon
Call our kings and heroes. Send
For great Achilles!

ODYSSEUS

No!

AJAX

No.

ODYSSEUS

Be silent
I am no fool.

AJAX

Foolish plans
Come from foolish heads.

ODYSSEUS

Take that back, Ajax!

AJAX

I speak my mind.

ODYSSEUS

And I can.
Speak with my own sword!

CHORUS OF SOLDIERS

Down. Be silent you
Or bring our angry foes to
Our camp, to our deaths.

AJAX

Our deaths are on us.

CHORUS OF SOLDIERS

Put out the flames or the fire
Will lead them to us.

ODYSSEUS

No! Wait! These small flames
Won't be seen by eyes used to
Brilliant city lights.

These fires are a few
Among many of our host.
They may pass us by.

AJAX

They may.

ODYSSEUS

They will. I
Won't die by these chilly flames.
They will pass us by.

Trust that I am right.

AJAX

It would be the first time this
Night that you were so.

ODYSSEUS

I told you.

CHORUS OF SOLDIERS

Quiet!
Is that them?

ODYSSEUS

Who?

AJAX

Where are they?

ODYSSEUS

Is but a shadow.

CHORUS OF SOLDIERS

Are you sure?

ODYSSEUS

I am.
See the flickering prick of
Flame beyond that wall.

The flame is so small
That is makes the tiny bench
Seem as a great beast.

CHORUS OF SOLDIERS

Do you not hear them?
The coming of a great host?

ODYSSEUS

Silent and listen!

AJAX

Do you hear them?

ODYSSEUS

No.
But wait—

AJAX

Pull back to shadow—

ODYSSEUS

It's a pissing dog.

CHORUS OF SOLDIERS

A dog! Hapless hound
That follows our camp looking
For scraps of food.

Food! I've not eaten
Real meat for many months. Then
We can dinner now!

Here dog! Here dog! Ho!

ODYSSEUS

Be still and silent as graves;
Tell them not we're here

You can dine or die!

AJAX

I do not think we're enough....
If they find this camp.

ODYSSEUS

They will not see us.

AJAX

We need more men.

CHORUS OF SOLDIERS

Yes, we do
Call out for more men.

ODYSSEUS

At last be silent!

AJAX

No one comes.

ODYSSEUS

I think so, too.

AJAX

P'raps they fear a trap.

ODYSSEUS

It is certain they
Aren't afraid of our soldiers,
Brave cowardly men

Who cower out of
The glow of the weak flames there.

CHORUS OF SOLDIERS

Fire burns.

ODYSSEUS

The dark hides!

AJAX

I say no one comes.

ODYSSEUS

And I agree. But he's there.
What is he doing?

AJAX

He gloats over the
Flesh of fallen Patroclus
Our dead comrade, there.

ODYSSEUS

He is mocking us.
What, far-seeing Ajax, do
You see in fire's glow?

AJAX

I see Hector stand
Over the body of the
Dead. He does nothing.

ODYSSEUS

He's a cruel bastard.
Does he not defile the dead?
Not strip the armor?

AJAX

He does naught but gaze
Up at the sky and count stars.
If I had a bow!

ODYSSEUS

Don't call attention
To us! What moves in shadows?
All's blur to my eyes.

AJAX

The shadows are black
But nothing blacker moves there.
No Trojan comes here.

CHORUS OF SOLDIERS
Then we are safe.

ODYSSEUS
For
Now. We are safe from Trojan,
Not from angry Greek.

AJAX
P'raps he'll understand.

ODYSSEUS
P'raps dogs will shit gold. Are you
Really such a fool?

AJAX
Not such fool as you,
Odysseus.

ODYSSEUS
What say you?

AJAX
You heard my words.

CHORUS OF SOLDIERS
Hush!

Do you want to wake
Achilles?

AJAX
I don't mind. 'Twas
Not my idea.

'Twas Odysseus
Who sent the old man to his
Death.

ODYSSEUS

How dare you say

You put blame on me?

AJAX

I did not dress the man in
Achilles' dread kit

ODYSSEUS

Do you say I did?

AJAX

Every man here knows you did.

CHORUS OF SOLDIERS

We saw you do it.

ODYSSEUS

Even Achilles
Must trust a chief before the
Common herd.

AJAX

I am

Not the common kind.
He will see truth in your eyes.
He'll venge Patroclus.

ODYSSEUS

No one who speaks will
Live to draw another breath.

AJAX

You'll die with sword sheathed.

He may not have your
Gift for thought, but passion and
Anger are faster.

ODYSSEUS

I will not take the
Fall alone. Achilles will
Kill all who helped me.

Friend Ajax, there's no
Comfort in dying alone.

AJAX

I want not to die.

ODYSSEUS

No more than do I
But give me time to think, I'll
See to all our lives

CHORUS OF SOLDIERS

Be silent great lords
For there is fire that comes now
From the Trojan walls.

They all go and watch

SCENE 3
The Battlefield
About the same time

HECTOR, as before, stands above the body of PATROCLUS

HECTOR

Who are you? That is
A fair question, so I ask.
You aren't Achilles.

It took a heartbeat.
No, even less, the flap of
A moth's wing as it

Takes flight to reach the
Flickering light that chases
Away the night's dark

To know you weren't he.
So what fool, what crazed hero
Would dare don that suit?

Armor a present
To your better from the gods
Themselves, so they say.

The air, clouds, and rain
Did not save your skin, hero.
Earth's steel took your life.

You deserved to die
You know. You're not Achilles.
You may frighten the young,

The callow will fly
Before your pathetic roars,
But I am no fool.

How dare you? You dared
To charge among foes not as
Man, but counterfeit.

Not brave enough to
Stand alone to face your death
With some dignity.

You puff out feathers
And bellow in a feigned voice,
Hope to frighten men.

Frighten boys. Frighten
Those who fear th'idea of
Death, not death itself.

Had you faced fought dared
Me as a man as yourself,
Perhaps you would live.

Perhaps I'd have slapped
You down as I would a child
Who had misbehaved.

You could cower in your
Hut afraid of moon's light beams
Afraid of night's life.

I shall unmask you.
Let Artemis judge your life
As I judged your death.

HECTOR unmasks PATROCLUS

Ah! That explains much.

PATROCLUS

I did not expect to die.

HECTOR

To be killed so soon.

You are younger than
We'd thought for one who'd unmanned
The great Achilles.

And now, man, unmanned
Your shade awaits transport to
Your Elysian rest.

PATROCLUS

There is no rest yet
For my journey is not done
Under sun's hot fire.

HECTOR

Apollo's light will
Not fill your heart nor warm your
Limbs.

PATROCLUS

Yet I am here.

HECTOR

Yet you are here. Why?

PATROCLUS

Perhaps to warn you of death.

HECTOR

When I saw your face,

That is when I knew.

PATROCLUS

Yet you are here. Why not fly?

                    HECTOR

Why not fly?

                    PATROCLUS

That's right.

                    HECTOR

Where?

                    PATROCLUS

Where?

                    HECTOR

Would I go?

                    PATROCLUS

Where?

                    HECTOR

Exactly.

                    PATROCLUS

Far from here.

                    HECTOR

The goddess lives in

These walls; I cannot,
Won't abandon her to your
Gods' rough caresses

                    PATROCLUS

They will win.

                    HECTOR

Perhaps.
However, I will not leave
No matter what.

PATROCLUS

Ah!

But whether or not
You stay, should you stand before
The city gates and

Shrug off the great waves
Of men like cliffs scoffing at
Neptune's storms and tides.

Time will out and, like
Stone, you will weary and fall
Like—

HECTOR

Then I will fall.

PATROCLUS

The great flame of Troy
Will be doused.

HECTOR

Light will find a
Way through darkest dark.

PATROCLUS

Troy's fire will be quenched.

HECTOR

All that needs to survive is
The smallest ember.

Look to our stars there
Wand'ring alone in heaven.
How apart are they.

They circle the skies
Searching for one another
And sometimes they meet.

And when they meet there
Is such a great burst of light
That the heavens glow.

P'raps that is our sun—
A thousand thousand tiny
Gods there embracing.

Perhaps that is Troy—
Thousands of men's lights, men's souls
Gathered for a time

Bringing brightest light
To glow as a great city
Warming divine earth.

PATROCLUS

Your mother earth will
Soon be merely an ember
Raped by the darkness.

The thunderclouds come
And will cover your land.

HECTOR

The
Winds may douse the light,

But the Trojan sparks
Will dance before the fell winds
And burrow in earth,

There to keep warm and
Wait for other Trojan sparks
And wait and gather

And phoenix-like burst
Into another great flame.
P'raps that is our fate.

PATROCLUS

That is not your fate.

HECTOR

Even gods don't know their fates.

PATROCLUS

A great burning comes.

You should prepare for
The approach of Achilles'
Flame, which comes for you.

Even if Troy lives
Hector's light will dim and die.
Achilles loves me.

His thunderstorm will
Come and drown the great Hector.

HECTOR

He may drown my light.

PATROCLUS

He will.

HECTOR

Then he will.
The gates of Troy are open
Women come for you.

PATROCLUS

Why?

HECTOR

We care for the
Dead.

PATROCLUS

Achilles would want to
See his dead lover.

HECTOR

We don't defile the
Dead. Fools or heroes are all
Honored in great Troy.

PATROCLUS

Achilles—

HECTOR

Can come
For you. We will not leave your
Body to the crows.

We are not Greeks.

PATROCLUS

He
Will want to honor me.

HECTOR

Who
Are you to the man?

Friend? Lover?

PATROCLUS

Teacher.
Man. I am all things to him.
But now I am dead.

HECTOR

But now you are dead.
Do Greeks love their dead so?

PATROCLUS

He
Would.

HECTOR

Achilles—

PATROCLUS

Yes.

HECTOR

Why not go to him?
P'raps his love will warm your death.

PATROCLUS

You don't understand.

HECTOR

I don't?

PATROCLUS

Achilles,
Beloved of the gods, will rage
And tear life and death.

HECTOR

You fear him.

PATROCLUS

I do.

HECTOR

But you are dead.

PATROCLUS

Death is naught
To great Achilles.

His anger will blast
The skies and make Olympus
Shudder from its strength.

It will shake the stones
And crack the mountains. I fear
For those who tell him

Fear him.

HECTOR

I will not.
So long as my feet stand on
Earth, I fear no man,

E'en if he kills me

PATROCLUS

Then, Hector, you are the fool.
Death will not save you.

His passions are hot
As death cold.

HECTOR

Passions wane.

PATROCLUS

But
First burn like the sun.

Look. Your friends come now
Followed shortly by a great
Blast of wrath and ire.

It comes heavy on
Air that fears to bear it. Soon
Your ears will hear what

My heart can hear now.
I fear the anger as much
As I love the man.

HECTOR

Bear him gently. Fool
That he might have been, he died
Braver than many.

*A great roar of a single-voice is heard from
the Greek camp*

Perhaps braver than
Even Hector will face doom.
Bear him with rev'rence.

We are Troy, not Greece.
Clean his wounds, clothe him not
In rags but fine silks,

For when Achilles
Comes to claim his lover then
Hector must not be.

And then in vengeance
Will Greek hordes break upon the
Walls of this fair town.

They, finding a chink
Not guarded by Hector, will
Pour in drowning all.

PATROCLUS

Do you follow us?

HECTOR

I will speak with wife and son.

PATROCLUS

Say son before wife.

HECTOR

I say wife first. I
Gave life to son, but first I
Gave my life to her.

PATROCLUS

A strange people, you.

HECTOR

No stranger are we to you
Than you are to us.

PATROCLUS

I am borne away.

HECTOR

There are people to the north,
Where winters are cool

And the sun lies low
Save for the hottest months, who
Take beloved dead

And cast them on a
Great river. Bodies float to
A great cataract

And then there plummet.
When one strikes the rocks below
A small spark flies loose

And denies Hades
Ownership of the dead's soul.
The spark then drifts back,

Hidden and waiting,
Until a cooing newborn
Baby first draws breath.

The spark then enters
And the soul once again grows.
Old souls in new lives.

I'm told by the priests
That the spark goes from body
To body ever.

PATROCLUS

What god decides where,
In what manner of person
Your spark reignites?

HECTOR

Not just man but in
Beast as well. No gods decide.
The fates judge our lives

And then they decide.
Am I fated to be a
Soldier forever?

Is Hector fated
To fight Achilles now and
Again and again?

Or will great Hector
Be nothing but a mewling
Cat, to stretch and yawn

While others fight and
Die? Where's greatness. Or's greatness
From living your life

With the cards dealt you?
Are the stars, the gods, merely
Waiting sparks of man

Looking, searching, for
A newborn worthy of them?
That deserves their light?

Will my spark, just out
Of reach, love my own son or
Fill my wife with warmth?

PATROCLUS

Come and love your son.
Hold your wife, fill her with warmth.
Do it while you live.

HECTOR

I wait Achilles
He could not kiss you goodbye.
Do I deserve more?

I await my fate.

PATROCLUS

Dead, I know this much of fate:
Achilles will come.

He will find you. Your
Death's as certain as mine. But
You can choose the time.

Come.

HECTOR

I come. How oft
Can a soldier find the chance
To bid love farewell.

They leave

SCENE 4
The Outskirts of the Greek camp
About the same time

*The Greeks are cautiously watching the
other parts of the offstage-Greeks' camps*

CHORUS OF SOLDIERS

Look at them. They will
Put out the fires before long.
Are they watching Troy?

Will they come? Will there
Be a counterattack?

ODYSSEUS

No.
They will not venture

Through their gates tonight
And approach our burning camps
Now that....

AJAX

Now that....

ODYSSEUS

Yes.

Even Hector must
Fear the wrath of Achilles.
But still he stands there.

AJAX

If we could take him,
P'raps that would calm Patroclus'

Lover of his wrath.

ODYSSEUS

Far-sighted Ajax,
Can you see so far as to
See if we could?

AJAX

No.

My sight is for the
Battlefield. My eyes cannot
See to tomorrow.

ODYSSEUS

Could you take him?

AJAX

If
I had a strong enough bow,
No wind, he stood still.

ODYSSEUS

I don't think Hector
Will stand still and allow your
Arrow to hit him.

AJAX

What is your thinking?

ODYSSEUS

Not to come 'tween Achilles,
Hector, and vengeance.

CHORUS OF SOLDIERS

A sound plan that proves
Vulpine Odysseus is as
Clever as is said.

Let the winds carry
News of Patroclus' murder
To his fell lover.

Let Achilles rage
And storm the great walls of Troy
In search of Hector.

P'raps Odysseus'
Plan will bear fruit after all
And end this damn war.

Then we can return
To our homes and to our wives,
So long we've been gone.

ODYSSEUS

Many months will pass
Many fires of life be snuffed
Ere I return home,

Before I go to
See faithful Penelope,
Ere I see my son.

CHORUS OF SOLDIERS

Hector will die and

ODYSSEUS

The great flame of Ilium's
Fire will be but dimmed.

CHORUS OF SOLDIERS

Come, Odysseus,
Poets will sing tales of you,
Will recall that you

Manned Achilles and
Sent him against great Hector,
Who must surely die,

And all the wives and
Lovers from our distant hearths
Give you joyous praise,

Odysseus, and
Ajax, ever comrades, who
Brought down Troy's great walls.

Ajax and foxy
Odysseus together
Dragged, no, forced, no, tricked

The brooding hero
From his sweaty sticky cot,
The sullen hero

To kill the city's
Champion before her gates.
Odysseus and

Ajax will be known
As the saviours of Greece.

THERSITES

Ha!
What will they see but

Odysseus' and
Ajax' flayed naked husks there
Writhing in the dirt.

Do you think he's such
A fool, Achilles? Once his
Wrath against Hector

Is sated, he will
Remember who're the authors
Of his tragedy.

Will he thank you for
A lover's death? Will he think
Troy's fall worth his loss?

I think not.

ODYSSEUS

No one
Cares what Thersites thinks.

AJAX

What
Horrid beast is this

To question the ways
Of kings?

THERSITES

Not such a fool to
Kill Achilles' love.

Not such a coward
To hide and hope Patroclus'
Death goes unnoticed.

AJAX

Coward he calls us?
You wall-eyed dent-headed prat
To challenge us so!

ODYSSEUS

Who will notice your
Death? Who will avenge your death?

CHORUS OF SOLDIERS

This lump is nothing.

THERSITES

Brave 'nough to abuse
Malshapen me, but too scared
To face Achilles.

ODYSSEUS

What are you to him?
You dare even say his name!

THERSITES

Nay! Leave me be!

AJAX

Stay!

Wily Odysseus,
Think for a moment. Can you
Think of a better

Man to tell the sad
News to Achilles? Can you?

THERSITES

No!

ODYSSEUS

Of course.

AJAX

That's right!

ODYSSEUS

Why didn't I think
Of it?

AJAX

Perhaps you did.

THERSITES

No
It is not my place.

It's not my story.

ODYSSEUS

I've an idea, Ajax.

AJAX

Why, I'm not surprised

ODYSSEUS

Let Thersites go
And face a lover's anger.
Let Thersites die.

THERSITES

Perhaps I should leave.

AJAX

Stay! Invite him to sit down!

CHORUS OF SOLDIERS

Stay here by the fire!

THERSITES

But—

ODYSSEUS

No buts, dear friend.

THERSITES

I better trust the abuse.

ODYSSEUS

You should know the tale.

THERSITES

You sent Patroclus
To face great Hector, there he
Was killed by his foe.

Too many know of
Your plots and plans to doubt e'en
Achilles must know.

ODYSSEUS

Achilles will know
What Achilles is told. Give
Thersites some wine.

CHORUS OF SOLDIERS

Here!

THERSITES

I will not—

CHORUS OF SOLDIERS

Drink
It boy!

AJAX
(Overlapping)

Boy, listen.

THERSITES

No more.

ODYSSEUS

More!

AJAX

Wily Ithacan
Explain.

THERSITES

Let me go!

ODYSSEUS

Quiet!
Achilles will know

What you tell him.

AJAX

You
Will go to Achilles' tent
And pass by his whore.

Tell him the story
Of his lover's murder—

THERSITES

And
Die for the telling.

ODYSSEUS

More wine!

THERSITES

No!

CHORUS OF SOLDIERS

Yes!

ODYSSEUS

Not
Die.

AJAX

Achilles won't kill you.

THERSITES

He will.

ODYSSEUS

He'll thank you.

CHORUS OF SOLDIERS

More wine!

THERSITES

More wine!

ODYSSEUS

Get
Another flask; make it two.

AJAX

Or three.

THERSITES

Four. To die!

ODYSSEUS

P'raps a little death.

AJAX

A gift from hot Achilles
To the messenger.

ODYSSEUS

Cajole Achilles.

THERSITES

Cajole Achilles.

ODYSSEUS

Shame him.
Why'd Patroclus die?

THERSITES

Why indeed?

ODYSSEUS

Fast-tongued
Thersites can surely out
Think dull Achilles.

THERSITES

What should I say?

ODYSSEUS

Who
Are we to put honeyed words
In so skilled a mouth?

AJAX

Your dexterous tongue shall
Sway Achilles' blackened mood.

ODYSSEUS

He will thank you.

AJAX

We!

We will all thank you
You'll be known as....

ODYSSEUS

Thersites....

AJAX
(To ODYSSEUS)

Is that all you've got?

ODYSSEUS
(To AJAX)

Aye, it is.

CHORUS OF SOLDIERS

More wine!

THERSITES
(With Chorus of Soldiers)

More wine!

ODYSSEUS

Thersites the Golden Tongued!

AJAX

Achilles'll like that!

ODYSSEUS

Shut up.

AJAX

Go on.

ODYSSEUS

Who
Dared the very Trojan fires....

AJAX
(To ODYSSEUS)

"Very Trojan fires"?

THERSITES

Very Trojan fires!

ODYSSEUS
(To AJAX)

See.

THERSITES

I'm pretty brave!

AJAX

Just so!

ODYSSEUS

To....

AJAX

To....

CHORUS OF SOLDIERS

To?

THERSITES

To!?!?

ODYSSEUS

To

Bring...back...something....

AJAX

What?

ODYSSEUS

To bring back a braid of hair.

THERSITES

A braid of whose hair?

ODYSSEUS

Patroclus' hair, fool!

CHORUS OF SOLDIERS

Of course. To show Achilles.

THERSITES

Why show him some hair?

ODYSSEUS

Don't ask me. You are
The one who went back for it.
To take to his tent.

THERSITES

To take to whose tent?

ODYSSEUS

Have we given him too much?

CHORUS OF SOLDIERS

Not nearly enough.

More wine!

THERSITES

Yes, more wine!

ODYSSEUS

To take to Achilles' tent.
You know. His lover.

THERSITES

Yes, Patroclus' love
Or is it Achilles' love

ODYSSEUS

No matter!

THERSITES

The hair?

ODYSSEUS

What hair?

THERSITES

For which I
Dared the very fires of Troy
And chopped from dead's head.

ODYSSEUS

That hair. You must find
It before you reach his tent
Or he'll smell the lie

THERSITES

We wouldn't want that.

AJAX

No!

ODYSSEUS

No!

CHORUS OF SOLDIERS

Of course not.

ODYSSEUS

Never!
But you must go now!

They push him out

AJAX

Don't forget to find
The hair! Did Patroclus braid
His hair?

ODYSSEUS

We'll find out.

SCENE 5
Achilles' Tent
Shortly After

ACHILLES is abusing BRISEIS

THERSITES enters

THERSITES

My lord Achilles.
My lord.

BRISEIS

What is it? Speak, man.
Achilles listens.

THERSITES drinks

THERSITES
(Aside)

How shall I tell this
Story? Was Patroclus the
Hero of this tale?

Did he don the suit?
Did he fight the foe for his
Glory and for ours?

To die for glory.
Will such a death appeal to
Patroclus' fell love?

Was Patroclus the
Doddering fool, desperate
Once more to trod the

Stage of battle, to
Put on a mask of greatness
To feign life ere death

Closed the curtains on
His weakened frame? One last roar
To be drowned by the

Sound of its horrid
Terrorful sequel that must
Tell a greater tale.

A tale of better
Men, of heroes loved by gods
Perhaps feared by them,

Not pathetic old
Boy-fellating men. No great
Heroism in this.

Will Achilles praise
The bearer of such tidings?
Does he want to hear?

Yet hear he must.

BRISEIS

He
Awaits whatever news you
Are bringing to him.

Lame Thersites! My
Master holds no love for you.
His patience wears thin

THERSITES

I speak; I will speak
By and by. Whom should I fear
More, master or whore?

BRISEIS

Speak!

THERSITES

Of course, lady.
First more wine. My golden tongue
Seems to have failed me

BRISEIS

Speak!

THERSITES

Should I say that
Patroclus was the dupe to
Odysseus' fox?

A fool to mock his
Betters. But a weakling to
Imitate the strong.

Did he imitate?
Did he mimic? Who was fooled?
Did Trojans fly in

Fear? Did Greeks rally?
Breach the unbreachable walls?
Chase our foes away?

Dupe or not, a fool
To ruse Hector, fool to die.
Tell Achilles that!

Clever Thersites,
Misshaped thoughts from misshaped form.
Will ugliness save

You from his swift sword?
Has beauty saved Briseis
From Achilles' thrust?

Did Aphrodite's
Beauty save Troy's future from
Greece's Armada?

Fire burns when and where
It will; men and gods will die
When the fates so will.

Can I sidestep fate?
Can I dodge Achilles' blade?
Should I even try?

BRISEIS

Achilles would have
You speak.

THERSITES

When I am ready.
When I am ready.

BRISEIS

He's a bold monster.

THERSITES

Wine - or fear - have made me brave.
Think fast! Fool or dupe?

Hero or scapegoat?
Tragedy or comedy?
Odysseus' plot

Is life, death f'r'us all.
Should I soak the tale in wine
To kill bitter taste?

There is not enough
Honey in all of these lands
To sweeten this death.

Take a deep breath, now
Let your wine-fueled golden tongue
Tell this sad story.

Let Achilles know
That I cared so to soften
The blow of this news.

BRISEIS

Speak now!

THERSITES

Patroclus
Is dead! Oh, crap! That was smooth
To make so gentle

Such rough news.

BRISEIS

Repeat.
Again.

THERSITES

I dare not!

BRISEIS

Do it!

THERSITES

I fear—

BRISEIS
(overlapping)

Fear death not truth

THERSITES

Patroclus fallen!
Counterfeiting Achilles.
Cut down by Hector.

BRISEIS

Beloved cousin!

THERSITES

Most cruelly did strike him down
Strike Patroclus down.

BRISEIS

I don't believe you.
Why would he kill that old man?
What had Patroclus

Ever done to him?

THERSITES

Why question cruelty, fury?
Why question envy?

BRISEIS

Envy?

THERSITES

Yes. Envy.
It was love of Achilles
Drove him to murder

Most brutally frail
Patroclus beloved by the
Great hero himself.

That is why, as we
Speak, Hector so abuses
Patroclus' remains.

He unmans the man,
There unmanning Achilles.
Otherwise why kill,

Why kill Patroclus?
Whom did the counterfeit fool?
Did it fool the Greeks

Who rallied to save
Him? Who braved the maddened wrath
Of Patroclus' bane

If only to save
The marred and the ravaged corpse
From Hector's rough lust?

I can see it now.
Hector's smirking snarling face,
His lips curled, sneering

Through his gritted teeth,
Patroclus covered with spit
And filth as they squat

Over him, laughing
At the humiliation
Of Achilles' love.

They mock you, my lord.
They savage Patroclus. They
Dance on his soul; they

Drink his blood; they gnaw
On his flesh and call it you.
To them you're nothing,

An effeminate joke.
Joke. Not hero. Not a man.
A callow virgin.

I watched them as he—
As Hector abused you, lord.
Even used your name.

To him Patroclus
Was nothing. No name, no man,
A convenient sheath

For his throbbing blade.

BRISEIS

For gods' sake be quiet, fool!
Can't you see his pain?

ACHILLES howls

THERSITES

My very heart quails
At such a sound; I must flee.

BRISEIS

Stay and stand you fool

THERSITES

Wherefore should I stay?
Achilles is unhinged, would
Kill innocent me.

Why should Thersites
Die for Hector's sin? Hector!
He's the one to die!

BRISEIS

Hector is merely
A soldier. Is he guilty
Of anything else?

THERSITES

Someone must pay for
Patroclus' death. It's Hector,
My lord, he's to blame.

BRISEIS

Did you stand with him?
Did you put yourself before
Him? Did you face death?

Did Patroclus die
Alone?

THERSITES

He did not. I dared
The battle's fury.

I could not save his,
Your, armor, but I did try,
Was able to get

A part, a relic
Cut from under the very
Nose of fell Hector.

This is all I could
Save of your glorious friend.
I brought it for you

What is going on?
Why does Achilles not move?

BRISEIS

When he is ready.

THERSITES

He has been unmanned.
He has been paralyzed. He
Is in shock.

BRISEIS

Not so.

He is surprised. He
Is furious. My master

THERSITES

Sits and stares at hair.

BRISEIS

You forget yourself.
My master and my cousin...
One will die tonight.

My Lover? Cousin?
Two sparks will meet and glow so
Brightly as to blind

Simple mortals like
Us. But in the end, one must
Be snuffed. Must darken

And cool, never to
Warm a soul a body, laugh
Cry eat or make love.

I would pray that they
Both fear death fear the darkness
The long road to hell

Where they will surely
Be prey to all their victims,
To all their lives' sins.

THERSITES

So long as the road
Is not haunted by me, they
May wander at will.

They can fight and kill
One another to their hearts'
Contents. I care not.

ACHILLES howls

BRISEIS

Hush.

THERSITES

Why?

BRISEIS

Don't you see?
My master prepares to go
And seek his vengeance.

THERSITES

His vengeance on whom?

BRISEIS

I would that he venge himself
On all that he meets

And douse the flaring
Light of his anger before
It engulfs my home.

He stands. I fear this
Greek for no man yet alive,
Lover or foe, can

Stand up to him.

THERSITES

I
Would not dare.

BRISEIS

I must flee for
I can't bear to watch.

BRISEIS flees deeper into the tent

THERSITES

And I must cower

He does

THERSITES

And pray Achilles passes
Me.

ACHILLES leaves

THERSITES

Praise gods he did.

*As if an afterthought, ACHILLES steps
back in and kills THERSITES*

SCENE 6
The Walls of Troy
Shortly After

HECTOR stands alone and looks out towards the Greek camps

HECTOR

So many lights. So
Many men. Tiny sparks that
Falter and sputter

Twirl, crash, and flare and
Burn out in but a moment
When they stand alone.

There is no love lost
For their fellows, for their kin.
They seem happiest.

Their days spent killing
Each other. We reap good from
This self destruction.

We grow strong and
More secure. We build our walls
'Round bright lit cities.

We learn to sing and
Dance and laugh and love, keep our
Women and daughters

Alive and teach our
Sons to put away their swords
And be civilized.

We laugh at distant
Sparks so far, so far away
As they pop and flash

And then disappear.
They give no light nor no heat.
How can they hurt us?

Why should we fear them?
But it is our fault when they
Gather together.

We should have watched them.
We should have seen them coming.
Is it now too late?

The sputtering spark
Feeds from Greek fuel and then bursts
Into inferno.

It can engulf us,
Threatens to. Can we stop it?
Should we even try?

The brightest light must
Dim. The greatest empire fall.
Men whither and age,

Then to be reborn.
Troy has not been forever.
Cannot always be.

PRIAM enters

PRIAM

It is the nature
Of all great men to become
Complacent and proud.

That is when they fall.

HECTOR

Father.

PRIAM

Son. I fear for you

HECTOR

And I for all Troy,

For should I fall....

PRIAM

For
Should you fall, who will lead our
City then?

HECTOR

You're king.

PRIAM

King, yes. Leader, no.
For I was born to the crown,
But you have seized the

Hearts of our people.
I did not expect this; I
Lived a life of peace,

But war came to us
I was ill prepared for it
I was a king of

Charts and of ledgers
I was happiest with trade,
Negotiations

Drawing borders on
Maps, sitting in judgment, in
Council. That is what

Being a king is.
You are a gen'ral at war.
You will never know

Lowering taxes,
Rights of way, or building codes.
You'll know only war.

You'll be remembered
For war.

HECTOR

I understand. That
Is the life I know.

PRIAM

I wish that you could
Be remembered as a king
Of peace who died old.

I bad you farewell
When you toddled off to school
All tears and sniv'ling.

HECTOR

And held my hand when
The slave gathered my things and
Carried me outside.

I was scared.

PRIAM

You kicked
And screamed. You mother thought that
I was beating you.

HECTOR

That you never did.

PRIAM

You were little. I worried
That I would mar your

Perfect form. Such a
Pretty child. By the time you
Were twelve, I could not.

You were too smart. I
Could not catch you in a lie,
And you were too strong.

E'en then, a soldier
Already a man to be
Reckoned with by men

Older, experienced.
More than others of your years.
You were better than

You had right to be.

HECTOR

I wanted to make you proud.

PRIAM

You've always done so.

HECTOR

It is not your way
To come bid farewell to your
Men before battle.

PRIAM

Is it your way to
Stick your head in the maw of
An angry tiger?

HECTOR

Perhaps in his rage
This great cat will misstep and
Lose his balance.

PRIAM

No!

Put not there your faith
Do not trust the beast to err.
Do not count on that.

I may not be a
Soldier. My life was not spent
With sword, spear, and shield,

But I have seen too
Many battles, many men
Fall—both friend and foe.

These Greeks are not men,
Don't fight like men think as men
They are destruction.

And Achilles is
The worst because he is best.
No life there, but death.

No mercy, but death.
No love there but of killing.
We should all fear them.

HECTOR

You would I fear him.
Achilles. I do. But fear
Should not hinder me.

Fear should never stop
Any man, let alone me.
I'll face Achilles.

Don't ask me to run.

PRIAM

Don't misunderstand me, I
Don't want you to flee.

As much as it would
Grieve me to see you fall, you
Can't avoid this fight.

These Greeks are beasts who
Want nothing but destruction
They'll turn Troy to dust,

Rubble if they can.
What will they put in its place
If they win? Nothing!

They are rabble! Troy's
A great city. Will the Greeks
Build another one?

Where are the glories
Of their lands? Their gods are mean
And petty. Do they

Build great tow'rs to
Reach the heavens? Are there proud
Poets who sing of

Their heroes' great deeds?
Their songs are doggerel; not
Palaces, mud huts.

We are part of an
Empire that stretches from the
Frozen mountains down

To the tropic seas.
Who are these Greeks to come here
Beach their ships, build their

Camps, steal our crops, take
Women, kill sons, burn cities
And destroy our lives?

Who are these villains?
Base and vile they are. How can
They be beating us?

I love you, Hector.
You are the child of my youth,
Of the great passion

That I had for your
Mother. The son of my hopes
The son of my dreams,

Of optimism
Of joy. With you I have had
So much happiness.

I don't want you to
Go and fight this monster; I
Don't want you to die.

But go you must, and
If die, then die you must for
They must be stopped now.

If Troy falls, then fall
It must, for they must be stopped,
Stopped ere they move on.

This is an empire
Great in peace and in culture
Bright with living gods,

Gods of hearth and root.
Are we to fall, be destroyed,
By these weak godlings

Of air and cloud and
Gusting winds? Perhaps, I fear,
We are. We're the end,

And the Greeks and he,
Achilles the destroyer,
Come to conquer us

And kill time and dance
On the back of the carcass
Of what once was great.

Perhaps Troy must fall.
Perhaps all of us must die.
P'raps that is our fate.

We can't avoid it.
But we don't have to like it,
To lie back and die.

You must stand before
Achilles' fury and say,
"No more, death bringer!

"Go back whence you came;
Leave Troy and her people at
Peace!" You must say that.

Though I fear he will
Not listen. Thoughts of peace are
Alien to his kind.

So you must fight him.
You must stand and face our fate.
Perhaps you will win.

HECTOR

Perhaps I will die.

PRIAM

Then I will weep over your
Body and pray that

The gods were pleased with
Your life and will send you back
To a better place,

A happier time,
Far far away from this flood
Of barbarians.

And if you beat him,
If you kill Achilles, all
The Greeks will depart.

I love you, Hector.
You are the son I wanted
To comfort me in

My old age, to care
For Troy after I became
Too old and infirm.

I had always dreamed
That you would live forever,
But that cannot be.

Your fate was not to
Be a man of peace, but to
Live and die in war.

HECTOR

Father.

PRIAM

Embrace me.
Kiss me and go on your way.
I believe in you.

And I pray that you
Can stop this inferno of
Greeks from wasting this

Land, devouring its
Cities, and destroying its
People.

HECTOR

I will try.

PRIAM

Face this Achilles
Bravely.

HECTOR

I'll do my best. I'll
Die fearing no man.

But Andromache,
My wife, facing her I fear
The tears of my son.

PRIAM

I would rather face
The fury of the Greeks than
The tears of a wife.

I'll watch the battle
From these walls with the women
Of our bright city.

You will no doubt see
Andromache and your boy,
Astynax, are near.

Embrace them, but do
Not linger. Achilles waits.
I go, boy, before

I stop you. I go.

HECTOR
Before, though, one last embrace.
Goodbye, dear father.

PRIAM leaves

*ANDROMACHE comes in with
ASTYNAX*

ASTYNAX
Daddy!

HECTOR
You should be
In bed.

ASTYNAX
There is so much noise.
Is there an attack?

Are we in danger?

HECTOR
This war is not your concern.
Don't fret over it

ASTYNAX
Mommy was crying.

HECTOR
Was it your mother or was
It you? Listen, son—

ASTYNAX

I went to the walls
Today. I liked watching the
Horses as they ran.

They go so swiftly.
Our men are better riders.
Braver than our foes.

HECTOR

No. Say not 'braver'.
There is no glory, honor,
In killing cowards.

Let Greeks be brave; let
Them be strong for they've slain
Many of my friends.

ASTYNAX

You are the bravest.
Ev'ryone tells me what a
Great warrior you are.

Even Achilles
Must fear you, with you sharp sword
And your bright armor

HECTOR

You used to cry when
I prepared for battle.

ASTYNAX

That
Was when I was young.

HECTOR

This war's first victim
Was childhood. So many homes
Filled with tears and cries,

Our rivers so clogged
With the bodies of our dead,
Eyes, with widows' tears.

HECTOR...

ASTYNAX

I do not cry now.

HECTOR

No, you don't.

ASTYNAX

With pride I watch
As you take your place.

I watch as you don
Your shining suit of mail and
Face the might of Greece.

Perhaps, someday, I
Will follow you to battle
Bearing sword and shield.

HECTOR

No!

ASTYNAX

I'm already
The best among the boys of
My age.

HECTOR

Again, no!

ASTYNAX

But father—

HECTOR

No! No!
I do not want my son to
Be a warrior.

I did not raise you
To be a killer of men,
Enemies or no

                        ASTYNAX

I must avenge the
Fathers, brothers, of my friends.
It is my duty.

                        HECTOR

No! Your duty is
To live. No! Your duty is
To father children,

To raise them far from
The roar of weapons, the clash
Of dying men. No!

                        ASTYNAX

Have I offended
You, father?

                        HECTOR

No, I am proud
As can be of you.

                        ASTYNAX

Then why? Why deny
Me the right to be a hero
Like my own father?

                        HECTOR

No. Not. Not deny.
Remember last winter when
We went to the hills?

                        ASTYNAX

Together we sneaked
Through the gates in the bitter
Night and made our way

Unseen across the
Great plain drenched in the blood of
So many great men.

                    HECTOR

We could see Greek fires.

                    ASTYNAX

We could hear the horses wheeze
And smell cooking meat,

                    HECTOR

And we went to the
Mountains, to that small cabin.

                    ASTYNAX

We stayed there for days

And hunted for food
And fished and e'en splashed our feet
In the freezing stream.

We huddled by the
Fire in the night and listened
To the winds outside.

                    HECTOR

Do you remember
The hawk?

                    ASTYNAX

That circled above
Then swooped and then dove.

                    HECTOR

What was he after?

                    ASTYNAX

I remember that he was
Hunting a rabbit.

HECTOR

That's right.

ASTYNAX

And he did
Not ever catch that rabbit.

HECTOR

Why couldn't he, though?

ASTYNAX

The rabbit would feed
And play by the stream. Above
The hawk would circle.

The rabbit would scratch
Itself on the hillock. The
Hawk would start to swoop.

The rabbit would doze
By an Ironwood tree. The
Hawk would swiftly dive.

A deadly arrow
Sublimely aimed as it flew
Straight at the target,

Aimed as true as Zeus'
Thunderbolt as fast as fleet-
Footed Mercury.

What a wond'rous sight.
And there, down below, it sits—
The helpless rabbit.

Doomed from the moment
The hawk started his fell dive.
Dead but not yet dead

It sits and dozes,
Perhaps enjoying a soft
And warm gentle breeze.

Maybe it can hear
With its long ears the light of
Armies by the sea.

It cannot know that
Its last thoughts before death will
Be of others' deaths.

And still the hawk comes
Screaming silently through the
Air. Faster! Faster!

Does the rabbit taste
The blood of dying Trojans
And Greeks in the air?

Does it hear their screams
Drifting by, following souls'
Journeys to Hades?

Does a spark from a
Dead brush its fur or tickle
Delicate whiskers?

Or is it the fates
Rewarding a good deed from
A previous life,

Or punishing a
Sin from the hawk's future, but
Suddenly it turns

And then disappears
Into its warren to scoff
And laugh at the hawk.

And the hawk cartwheels
And scrabbles at the wind to
Claw its way back up.

And then it circled
And waited for the rabbit.
And the rabbit came

Out into the weak
And feeble sun to feed and
To scratch and to doze.

And the hawk circled.
And it swooped and dove and missed
Again and again.

By and by the hawk
Tired and left, else it would die.

HECTOR

And the rabbit lived.

ASTYNAX

Until it's caught by
Another hawk or wolf or
A snake crawls into

Its cave and crushes
Its wives and young. In the end
It will always lose.

HECTOR

That is not so, boy!
A rabbit lives and loves and
Nurtures its fam'ly.

A hawk scavenges
And starves. It may be fast, strong,
And magnificent,

But it lives alone.
It dies alone. No chicks, no
Mates mourn its passing.

The hawk dies withered,
And its own kind feed on his
Carcass. Putrid. Dead.

ASTYNAX

It's magnificent.

HECTOR

It's vile, disgusting. Don't be
The hawk, Astynax.

Be the rabbit, son.

ASTYNAX

The rabbit?

HECTOR

Yes, the rabbit.
To be a soldier,

It is a grand life.
Not knowing what errant blade
Or stray arrow will

Bring you down, what far
And distant land will house your
Corpse. Who will weep then?

Who'll give your body
To the river gods or will
Leap onto your pyre?

Don't be the hawk; don't
Be the warrior.

ASTYNAX

I would
Follow my father.

HECTOR

I would you follow
Your mother! Without, there is
An army of hawks

Splendid in their gear
They would swoop and dive, destroy
Troy and her children.

You must burrow, hide,
Wait for them to starve and die.
Then you will be safe.

ASTYNAX

Until the next hawk.
The Greeks will never stop their
Quest to kill us all.

HECTOR

It is not a quest
It's merely a hungry tide.

ASTYNAX

Then why don't you hide?

HECTOR

I was not made for
Such a life, to my regret.
A man makes a choice.

I chose to die young
So that my city could thrive
And last forever.

Somehow it will.

ASTYNAX

I
Will sacrifice my life, too.

HECTOR

No! No! You must run.

Please, gods, you must run.
Heed me.

ASTYNAX

Father, why deny
Me of this same right?

If I must flee, you
Must as well.

HECTOR

Someone must stem
The Greek tide. Perhaps

If I slay the dread
Achilles, the tide will be
Slowed.

ASTYNAX

And if you fall?

HECTOR

That is what you fear?

ASTYNAX

My dreams are marred by nothing
Less. I fear the sleep,

Filled with dark nightmares
Of days when mother and I
Must fend without you.

Would you leave me? Would
You leave your little boy. I
Must know, father. Speak.

                    HECTOR

Do not shed tears for
Your father, living or dead.
Come to me, boy.

                    ASTYNAX

Do not want to lose
My daddy, not for Troy or
For the whims of fate.

                    HECTOR

You will never lose
Me. Dry your cheeks. Know that I
Will watch you ever.

A moment ago
I embraced my father; now
You must embrace yours.

Kiss me and farewell.

                    ASTYNAX leaves

                    ANDROMACHE
You should stay here with your son.

                    HECTOR
I've since bade you 'bye.

                    ANDROMACHE
It's been minutes since
Your last embrace, your last kiss,
And it seems like days.

Hold me once again
My husband, my lover. Oh,
Stay here tonight. Here

Inside the high walls.
Let the Greek rail at the stones.
Let him beat the air.

Let him slay the wind.
Let my husband stay alive
And come home with me.

Since I last saw you,
I have already died a
Thousand deaths and more.

Come with, fly with us
Take us to the mountains; take
Us to the deserts.

Desert this foul place
That stinks of death and deafens
Us with widows' cries.

Ten years have you fought,
Longer than our son has breathed.
This war has taken

You from your fam'ly,
From your home and those you love.
Isn't that enough?

We love each other.
That is enough for one man.
That should be enough.

Just the three of us:
A love, no battles, killings
A quiet old death

In my loving arms.
Hand in hand with loving son,
None else need be there.

Let Priam's Troy fall.
Let the Greeks burn the city
And steal its treasures.

I do not want rank.
I do not need power or
Silks, gold, even slaves.

I need my husband.
Astynax needs his father
To watch over him.

Find someplace, a land
The Greeks have never heard of,
That they'll never find.

That is where we'll live.
We can found another Troy,
And you can die a

King, husband, father
Lover. You can hunt for food.
We will till the soil.

Then your grandchildren
Can grow up not knowing war
Tears sorrow or blood.

Heed my pleadings, dear
Husband. Let me rule in this.
Listen just this once.

HECTOR

How can you ask this?

ANDROMACHE

Because I love you, need you
And your warm embrace.

HECTOR

An embrace that must
Grow cold should I abandon
The people of Troy,

The people who have
Loved me and given me trust.
I owe much to them.

ANDROMACHE

You owe them nothing.
What duty's there to those who
Expect you to die?

You've protected them,
You've spilled blood for them. Avoid
At least this one fight.

HECTOR

If I can't stop him,
Stop Achilles, who then will
Stem the flood of Greeks?

Who will keep safe our
Women and our children from
The vicious horde there?

Who will protect our
Allies, our lords? Someone must
Stop them—stop them now.

ANDROMACHE

And that someone must
Be you?

HECTOR

Yes.

ANDROMACHE

No!

HECTOR

I say yes!

ANDROMACHE

I, your wife, say no!

This Achilles, this
Beast, can kill another prince.
Priam has many,

I only have one.
This monster has killed before
My father, brothers.

All the family
Of my youth their souls cast from
The sunlight by him.

Because his rage burns
Fiercely, violently, now
I am an orphan.

Why should I give him
My husband? Should I offer
Him my son as well?

What is left for me?
What's left for Andromache?
Will he kill me next?

Think of me. Think of
Yourself. Think of your son and
Flee this place of death

Ere I cast myself
On the pyre set alight to
Send you to heaven.

HECTOR

Quiet! Be silent
Love. Kiss your loving husband
And then let me go.

I have a duty!
A duty! Hear me. It must
Come first. Before you,

Before family,
Before love. Do you doubt that
I would love to leave

These dark battlefields,
Leave this pain behind and take
You to a peaceful

Quiet life far from
Danger, care, and worries. But
I cannot, will not

Let this angry fire
Consume Troy. Whatever sins
Brought us to this place

Do not warrant so
Many deaths, so many tears.
I must try. I must.

Do not doubt my love—
A love that has warmed my heart
All these many years.

Do not be angry.
I may live; I may fall. Should
I fall, let me see

Your bright eyes love me
As they did the day we wed.
Let me carry the

Memories of their
Sparkle—those sparkles that lit
Up our nuptial bed.

Let me know you love
Me as you have these many
Years. Kiss me my love.

Your kiss will warm the
Steps I take to face my foe.
A kiss. An embrace.

Farewell my dear one.

He leaves

ANDROMACHE

And farewell to you, husband
Lover father friend.

PRIAM enters

PRIAM

Come, Andromache.
Take your young son to bed, then
Join me on the walls.

No tears, for Hector
Will ever be with us. We
Must be there for him.

Let your voice inspire
Him. Let your face lift his heart,
Your love protect him.

Sleep well, boy. Hector
Is a man like none other

ANDROMACHE and ASTYNAX
leave

PRIAM

Should he fall, we fall.

The light of Troy shines
In the hearts of her heroes.
The hearts of her sons.

If there is no light
Then the ravenous fire will
Win, will consume all.

PRIAM exits

SCENE 7
The Outskirts of the Greek Camp
Achilles' Tent
The Walls of Troy
The Battlefield
A short time later

> ODYSSEUS, AJAX, and the
> CHORUS OF SOLDIERS are
> *watching the battlefield*
>
> BRISEIS *sits on the floor of Achilles'*
> *tent.* THERSITES *(now a ghost) hovers*
> *around; his body has been covered*
>
> PRIAM *and the* CHORUS OF
> TROJAN WOMEN *are on the city*
> *walls*
>
> HECTOR *and* ACHILLES *are*
> *somewhere on the battlefield*

ODYSSEUS

All will be over.

AJAX

Soon, I trust, we'll hear Trojan
Women keening, and

Achilles will breach
The gates and we can enter.
It's because of us.

CHORUS OF SOLDIERS

What should I seek out
First? Gold or women? There will
Be plenty of both.

ODYSSEUS

We deserve credit
But the history books will
Write only of him.

AJAX

They'll only care for
Him—heroic Achilles,
Son of Peleus.

ODYSSEUS

Son of Thetis, say.
He's never credited his
Father much, not he.

CHORUS OF SOLDIERS

The younger ones put
Up much more of a fight than
The older ones do.

ODYSSEUS

What if Achilles
Were to die?

CHORUS OF SOLDIERS

Achilles's dead!

ODYSSEUS

No! No! He's not dead.

Go back to watching;
If he falls.

AJAX

He's a martyr.
So much worse for us.

Achilles has made
Enemies; we know to whom
To tell the story,

But dead—that's not good.
We must prefer him alive.
What did Thersites

Tell him?

ODYSSEUS

I don't know,
But when he came storming past
On his way out there,

He did not pause to
Kill any of us.

AJAX

Because
You were in hiding

ODYSSEUS

I was not hiding.
I was tying my laces.
And where was Ajax?

AJAX

Fetching his weapons
To follow Achilles, to
Stand with him against

Any Trojan tricks.

ODYSSEUS

Why aren't you with him?

AJAX

He's gone
On the battlefield.

ODYSSEUS

You could follow him.

AJAX

And be mistaken in the
Dark for his victim?

CHORUS OF SOLDIERS

Me? I was hiding.
Achilles might baulk before
He'd kill a great king

Such as your lordships.
But he would slaughter me with
Impunity, and

I saw his face when
He stormed from his tent, his face
Cloudy with anger

And loss. There was fire
In his eyes and his tears were
Like molten droplets.

Oh, yes. I hid. I
Hope for his sake Thersites
Did as well, poor man.

ODYSSEUS

And what of?

AJAX

What of?

ODYSSEUS
(To the CHORUS OF SOLDIERS)
Keep your eyes peeled for battle

(To AJAX)
Come here.

AJAX
What is it?

ODYSSEUS
She's there.

AJAX
Briseis?

ODYSSEUS
Yes. Young nymph.

AJAX
Ah!

ODYSSEUS
Worked in no
Doubt, but not....

AJAX
Too soiled.

ODYSSEUS
Distracted as he
Was by Patroclus' noble
Experienced charms.

She's inside.

AJAX
Waiting.

ODYSSEUS

No doubt. But does this trollop
Really care who comes?

AJAX

If Achilles finds
Out, he will surely kill us.

ODYSSEUS

Blame Agamemnon.

AJAX

Blame Agamemnon?

ODYSSEUS

Yes! It's dark. There is a mist
A girl goes missing.

We sneak in. Take her.
All eyes in the Greek camp are
Watching for Hector.

AJAX

To warn Achilles
Who does not need to be warned.
Should we go to her?

CHORUS OF SOLDIERS

Can you see something?

ODYSSEUS

Do you want to?

CHORUS OF SOLDIERS

Mist rises.
Was that a glint? There!

Moondust glancing off
A helmet or a shield. But
Whose helmet? Whose shield?

ODYSSEUS

Should he fall....

AJAX

Then we're
Closest to the tent and who
But Agamemnon

Would deny us a
Little reward for all our
Hard and tireless work?

For we'd....

ODYSSEUS

Have rid the
Camp of this brooding hero
Whose foul mood did suck

The warlike spirit
From our men—

AJAX

Gossiping old
Women to a man

CHORUS OF SOLDIERS

I can't see a thing.
Is there anything to eat?
Wake me when it starts.

ODYSSEUS

But should Achilles
Be victorious—there are
Many eyes about.

AJAX

Accidents happen.

ODYSSEUS

Not that many accidents.

AJAX

That is a pity.

She is ripe and my
Spirit ready to pluck her
Fruit.

ODYSSEUS

Mine, too. Pity.

CHORUS OF SOLDIERS

What was that?

AJAX

What?

CHORUS OF SOLDIERS

That!
He's seen him!

AJAX

Who has seen whom?

ODYSSEUS

Someone's seen someone.

AJAX

And so it begins.

ODYSSEUS

Good. I'm tired of waiting. Some
One must kill someone.

CHORUS OF SOLDIERS

Achilles will win.

AJAX

You think so?

CHORUS OF SOLDIERS

He's our best man.

ODYSSEUS

Hector knows the field.

CHORUS OF SOLDIERS

Five to one.

ODYSSEUS

Third pass.

AJAX

Sixth pass. I'll give Hector that.

CHORUS OF SOLDIERS

Sixth pass?

AJAX

Yes.

CHORUS OF SOLDIERS

All right.

> *Inside Achilles' tent, the Ghost of THERSITES stands; BRISEIS sits*

THERSITES

It's not so bad—death.
Not so much worse that living.
A bit colder, though.

Thank you for cov'ring
My face. I didn't want to
Look at it all night.

There's no one around
To bury poor Thersites.
All watch Hector's doom.

Why are you still here?
Woman!

BRISEIS

What?

THERSITES

Why are you here?
Why do you not run?

All the camp watches
Two great heroes do battle.
Now's the time to go.

Unseen you can slip
Between the lines and go home
To your family.

Go home to your friends

BRISEIS

I have no friends I have no
Family in Troy.

THERSITES

Have you a husband?

BRISEIS

He's dead. Killed by Achilles.

THERSITES

All the more reason—

BRISEIS

Have you taken a
Wife?

THERSITES

My ugliness denied
Me that great pleasure.

BRISEIS

You need a wife for
Pleasure? If that were so then
Slave girls would sleep more.

Surely, ghost, you have
Taken your pleasure on some
Hapless captive lass.

THERSITES

I'm but a common
Soldier. My obnoxiousness
Puts me last in line.

No pert young princess
Sent to share my bed and board.
I take my share of

Coin, and quaint reward
From the common whore. No great
Pleasures there for me.

BRISEIS

Your lack of care is

Better for the whore. She does
Not need to pretend.

She is free to loath
You, but the wife must love you
And show affection.

Myres, my husband,
Was an old man. Sure, he was
Kind enough, but old.

Where's the fun for a
Thirteen year old girl, flush with
Youth, ripe with passion?

To be saddled with
Someone who reminds her of
Her loving father.

I dreamed of princes
And got an arthritic king
Who wheezed and gasped and

Coughed when we made love.
I could not hate him. He did
Nothing to hurt me,

Loved me in his way.
I went from dolls to dotage
With nothing between.

I wept when he died,
My husband, when Achilles
Killed him. As I should.

It was my duty.
But then I also rejoiced.
A widow is free.

But war kills all the
Young men. I could not find my
Prince. They're all taken

By young gossiping
Virgins. They were consid'ring
Me for another

Husband.

THERSITES

Better than
Slavery.

BRISEIS

I disagree.

Say not 'better,' say
'Not all that different.' Where
Is my decision?

Why do you think I'm
Here?

THERSITES

You are Achilles' prize.

BRISEIS

Ha! Achilles' prize?

I am Priam's plot
Sent to distract Achilles.
A complication

To confuse your plans
And strategies. Surprising
How it was working.

How often do young
Princesses go alone to
Make sacrifices

So far from safety?
Under the noses of the
Enemy? Tell me.

But Hector loves me.
He would not have allowed this.
He would have stopped it.

Had he but known. Had
Priam confided in his
Greatest general,

I would not be here;
Patroclus would not have died;
And Hector would live.

THERSITES

So would Thersites

BRISEIS

Perhaps.

THERSITES

Still, it's not so bad
It's very quiet

BRISEIS

The noise will come soon.
The end means little to me.
No matter who wins,

I will still be here.
If Achilles falls, his friends
Will come and take me.

One tent must look like
Another.

THERSITES

P'raps Achilles
Will fall and the gates

Of Troy will open.
Your cousins, your lovers, will
Swoop down and save you

P'raps you'll be lucky.

BRISEIS

Perhaps you are right, But Greece
Has many heroes—

Had many heroes
Waiting to take the place of
Noble Achilles.

Troy has heroes, too.
Will Achilles kill them all?
One will get lucky.

Maybe, soon, all—all
Heroes will lose their light and
Will lie on blood-soaked

Corpse-darkened fields. Black,
Lifeless. And both Greece and Troy
Will hear women's cries,

Will hear women's sighs
And will no longer hear the
Clamor of battle,

The dying of youth.
Until then, I'm past caring.
Greek cot, a down bed

In Trojan palace
Will be my field of battle
Regardless who wins.

*PRIAM and the CHORUS OF
TROJAN WOMEN watch*

PRIAM

Can you see them yet?
The moon's nearly set, and the
Sun has yet to rise.

CHORUS OF TROJAN WOMEN

The moon still shines too
Brightly to make an old man
Handsome. I saw him—

I saw Hector ere
He went through the gates. Now there's
An attractive man.

Achilles is a
Bow-legg'd cretin, his armor
Dull and battle-worn.

He must be a brute.
You've heard the stories of him.
Poor, poor, Briseis.

Agamemnon has
No doubt a sumptuous tent.
Were I a captive

Better silken ropes
Than rough cot and caresses
Of an uncouth brute.

PRIAM

Quiet your prattle.
Prefer death to the darkness.

CHORUS OF TROJAN WOMEN

It's hard even to

Find a good slave girl,
So many soldiers about
In need of comfort.

Many rough peasants,
So few noble princes left.
What becomes of us

When this war's finished?

PRIAM

Hush, I say again. Good! Here
Comes Andromache.

CHORUS OF TROJAN WOMEN

I can't share my wine
With her. I've enough for me.
Had I days to plan

I could have prepared
Quite a feast for all of us.
It's so annoying.

ANDROMACHE

Here, father, I come.
Astynax is put to bed.
Would I were with him

PRIAM

Would you were with my
Son. To lie with Hector must
Be preferable

To these murky walls.

ANDROMACHE

I will lie with him tonight.

CHORUS OF TROJAN WOMEN

With him or alone

You will surely lie
Tonight. Menelaus is
Certainly handsome.

Why does he so moon
Over his trollop wife. And
Odysseus there

Is a handsome man.
What about Ajax, his friend?
Too short and too dark.

I fear the Greeks like
Their bed-mates hairy and male.
What's a girl to do?

ANDROMACHE

The mist is too thick.
I think I see someone there
Over by that stream.

PRIAM

I pray that stream's god
Loves us, will burst its banks, wash
Achilles away.

ANDROMACHE

I fear the gods will
Have no part in this fight; they
Have abandoned us.

PRIAM

Say not so. The gods
Have subtle hearing; they can
Hear a whispered prayer

'S'well as one bellowed.

ANDROMACHE

Then I must yell the louder
For them to notice.

Let Troy fall, but let
My husband live! Let Hector
Return to his wife!

PRIAM

Now, Andromache,
I understand how you feel,
But Troy must come first.

ANDROMACHE

Why?

PRIAM

Pardon?

ANDROMACHE

Why?

PRIAM

Why?

ANDROMACHE

Must Troy come first?

PRIAM

Troy is our
Mother and father.

It has nurtured us
Sheltered us, protected us
From wind, storm, rain, fire—

ANDROMACHE

When I wed, I left
My parents' house. Hector is
My protector now!

I don't see these walls
Sheltering him, protecting
Him from Achilles.

CHORUS OF TROJAN WOMEN

I think I see a
Glint of moonlight on burnished
Armor. Is it he?

Look there, a shadow
There moves nearer to Hector
From beyond that hill.

ANDROMACHE

Come, father, we don't
Have to watch. We can go home.
Win or lose, home is

Where we should be.

PRIAM

I'll
Stay. I watched Hector's first steps.
I watched his falls, I

Watched his scraped knees and
Bruised pride. What sort of father
Would I be if I

Could not watch his death.
On these walls, I have watched my
City grow, fam'ly

Rise. I have wept on
This place as my sons, the sons
Of my people fought,

Died these past ten years.
I have seen dark flames approach
These shores and threaten

To engulf my world.
This is a place of joy and
A place of sorrow.

If Hector, if he
Falls to Achilles' sword, then
I—king—must bear it.

And if Hector should
Win and slay this beast, then where
Else should I be? Where?

ANDROMACHE
You should be right here.

CHORUS OF TROJAN WOMEN
Hush! Hush! Something's happening!
Get out of the way!

> *HECTOR and ACHILLES meet on the field*

HECTOR
So, you're Achilles?
Would that I could say 'well met.'
We have yet to meet

On the field or in
The conference halls of great
Men. Yet, I know you.

Your reputation
Is broadly known. You have killed
Many of my friends,

Cousins, and comrades.
Go from this place, Achilles.
You can't kill us all.

> *They fight*

ODYSSEUS
Achilles will strike
Him down.

AJAX

It won't be long now.

ANDROMACHE

Live, my darling one!

Live, Hector.

PRIAM

Gods, hear
Our prayers. Let my son survive.

CHORUS OF TROJAN WOMEN

They're both handsome men.

I think Achilles
Is the taller, but look how
Hector's armor shines.

CHORUS OF SOLDIERS

Hector's too pretty
To be a great warrior.
Strike fast, Achilles!

THERSITES

Soon, your master will
Come.

BRISEIS

You say 'come,' not 'return.'

THERSITES

Does it matter much?

HECTOR

Can you kill us all?
Is that what you want? Is it?
What will you do then?

When Troy is no more.
Will you and your people move
On to the next place?

What will you have in
The end? Glory? Is it fame
That you are seeking?

By the time you are
Through—by the time you have killed
All of us—what's left?

All the poets will
Be dead. They'll be no one left
To sing your praises.

They fight

CHORUS OF SOLDIERS

Pay, Odysseus.
Hector still lives. Another
Wager. Four to one.

ODYSSEUS

Four to one?

CHORUS OF SOLDIERS

That's right.
Hector looks tired. He can't last
Very much longer.

AJAX

Hector's slippery.
Be careful, Odysseus
Or you'll soon be poor.

ODYSSEUS

I'll just steal again.
Plenty of soft cities that
Are within my reach.

If this rabble feels
That they can take me for more,
Then they'll follow me.

AJAX

You're a crafty man.

ODYSSEUS

Enough to go home richer
Than I was before.

CHORUS OF TROJAN WOMEN

Why do they take so
Long? They stop again.

PRIAM

What do
You women know of

The effort of war?
Battle is more exhausting
Than embroidering

Silk pillows in a
Gilded palace paid for with
The blood of brave men.

CHORUS OF TROJAN WOMEN

Brave words from Priam
Who huffs and gasps his way to
Hecuba's bed and

Humps her like a dog.
There's Hector! Looking this way.
Wave your scarf, your veil!

Get his attention!

ANDROMACHE

Do not distract my husband!
Rather, disturb the

Other man, his foe.
Remember you are Trojans
Not temple harlots

CHORUS OF TROJAN WOMEN

When it came time for
Her initiation, her
Ankles and her wrists

Were bound in strips of
Finest silver and Hector
Came as client and

Husband with payment
And dow'ry at the same time.
No slave soiled her flesh.

Her kind does not sit
And wait like a common whore.
Woo hoo! Hector! Here!

PRIAM

Ignore their clacking

ANDROMACHE

I always have done so.

PRIAM

Look
To your husband! There!

ANDROMACHE

Many times I've watched
Hector in battle. Never
Have I seen him face

His foe with such a
Cold, clear, calm, and resolute
Determination,

And he faces such
A wild and violent brute
That is Achilles.

PRIAM

Even in a beast,
There's oft majesty and grace
And nobility.

Were I a younger
Man, I'd face Achilles and
Spare Hector this fight.

ANDROMACHE

Were you a younger
Man, there would be no need for
This or any war.

Your bright mind and keen
Words would have sent these brutal
Greeks to hearth and home.

PRIAM

You flatter me.

ANDROMACHE

I
Have not the skill. Once you were
Considered among

The strongest greatest
Of kings. You're still a man of
Great virility.

PRIAM

Nonsense.

ANDROMACHE

I say so.
Those women may crab and gab
But secretly they

Wonder why you have
Not chosen one of them to
Ease your queen's burdens.

PRIAM

Come—with so many
Fierce and virile young soldiers
It would be unfair.

ANDROMACHE

Now I say 'nonsense.'
When this war's done—p'raps ere then—
I will help you look.

PRIAM

We should watch.

ANDROMACHE

Of course.

PRIAM

I worry Troy will not last.

ANDROMACHE

We must find a way.

HECTOR and ACHILLES fight

HECTOR

Where is the greatness
In your herd? From one city
To the next and next.

What does culture mean
To you? Civilization?
Art? Love? Beauty? Laws?

Should the world be just
A migrating mass of flesh?
Formless? Orderless?

PATROCLUS

Are you trying to
Convince him not to kill you?
I trust that won't work.

HECTOR

I do not plead for
My life, but to understand
The mind of my foe.

PATROCLUS

The mind of a 'brute'?
He is toying with you. Oh,
You'll die when he wills.

Just kill him, dear love.
Send him to me to torture
For eternity.

HECTOR

Is death so dull?

PATROCLUS

Yes.

HECTOR

I would our lives were as dull
As death seems to be

PATROCLUS

You'll find it dull as
Soon as you are dead.

HECTOR

I don't
Plan on dying soon.

HECTOR and ACHILLES fight

ANDROMACHE

He cannot weather
Such a brutal storm of blows.
Please open the gate!

CHORUS OF SOLDIERS

First blood! Achilles
Has scored a touch! A clear hit!
Yet Hector still fights!

BRISEIS

Is it done? Tell me

THERSITES

Blood's been spilt. No doubt ere it's
Over, both will bleed

Perhaps Briseis
Is torn. Who'd she rather dead:
Cousin or lover

BRISEIS

Would they both could live!
Would they both would die and leave
Briseis alone!

Whoever should die,
I am no prize. I shall not
Leave this tent, these shores.

I am uncommon
Slave for uncommon heroes.
I live so, die so.

ODYSSEUS

But he didn't fall!

AJAX

Pay up!

CHORUS OF SOLDIERS

First blood wins the bet.

AJAX

Ten says Hector's next

To draw blood.

CHORUS OF SOLDIERS

It is
Over.

ODYSSEUS

Don't throw away your
Money.

AJAX

It is mine.

What odds?

CHORUS OF SOLDIERS

Five.

ODYSSEUS

No. Ten.
I will win it back by dawn.

CHORUS OF SOLDIERS

Fifteen, I say.

AJAX

Done!

PRIAM

Open the gates? You!
Run down and bid them open
And let Hector in!

CHORUS OF TROJAN WOMEN

You go, Old Man! I
Would not miss this fight. It is
Not my son who'll die.

PRIAM

My legs have failed me.
Run, Hector! To the gates! Come
Home and live for now!

PATROCLUS

Why will you not die?
Achilles? Why won't you kill
Him? Strike him! Cut him!

HECTOR and ACHILLES fight

ASTYNAX sneaks onto the wall

PATROCLUS

Where is your rage? The
Ardor that should drive you to
Strike down my killer?

Now your blood mingles
With mine on his suit of mail.
Is that your plan? To

Die by Hector's sword?
I want vengeance, not your death.
Kill him! Kill Hector!

Achilles! Answer!
You are usually not
So close mouth'd—with me.

PRIAM

Are the gates open?

ANDROMACHE

The soldiers are distracted.

PRIAM

Oh, my goddess! Mine!

Divine Athena!
Resist the deadly push of
These barbarians.

Leave your unearthly
Pursuits and save Hector. Come
Down from the skies! Come

Down from the heavens
And strike down this maniac
Who threatens your slaves.

Oh, divine Hera!
See the plight of all mothers
Of all wives below.

What have they done to
Warrant the pains of loss these
Last ten years? Mother!

Mother to the gods,
Mother to us all, hear my
Cry. Ope your ears to

My supplication
And that of Andromache,
Eetion's daughter,

Hector's loving wife,
Mother of Astynax. Hear
Us! Accept our gifts

And sacrifices.
Save my son Hector. Hector
Who protects your priests

And women, temples,
Fields, and flocks. We beseech you.
Reach down and brush our

Enemies away.
Enemies who have tortured
And terrorized your

Faithful.

ASTYNAX

Father.

ANDROMACHE

Oh!

PRIAM

Divine Athena. Hear our
Prayer.

ANDROMACHE

Why are you here?

PRIAM

Protect your servant
Hector.

ODYSSEUS

Kill the bastard!

PRIAM

We
Have kept our faith with

You.

ASTYNAX

Father.

ANDROMACHE

Dear one
Keep quiet and go below!

PRIAM

We've kept ourselves pure.

Bring your thunderclouds.
Wash away this pestilence.
Make our country clean.

Chase our foreign foes
Back into the sea, back to
Their unworthy homes.

We've suffered enough,
Sacrificed. We have died to
Preserve your holy

Places. Hector now
Stands against an unholy
Enemy. Help him

Strike down Achilles.
Save my son, save my city,
Save my people, save

All your followers.

HECTOR

You may strike me down and leave
My carcass in the

Dust, but my spark will
Live on, will burn and someday
Will burst into flame.

My light and the lights
Of all the innocents you
Have murdered will one

Day blind you, eclipse
Your feeble barbarian
Inferno.

PATROCLUS

Strong words

From a corpse. He scoffs
At your pleas.

PRIAM

We've given you
Our blood and our faith,

You owe us your strength
And your loyalty. Without
Us you are nothing!

ASTYNAX

Father!

AJAX

Strike him down!

BRISEIS

Let it end.

THERSITES

Somehow, I thought
Death would hurt more.

AJAX

Die!

ANDROMACHE

Astynax, don't watch!

CHORUS OF TROJAN WOMEN

Why is that whining child here?

PATROCLUS

You can't run, Hector.

You can't avoid death.

HECTOR

Nor can Achilles.

ANDROMACHE

Run!

PRIAM

Flee!
The gates are open!

CHORUS OF SOLDIERS

Stop him! Achilles
Can storm Troy on his own.

ODYSSEUS

Suit
Up men! Make ready!

Achilles cannot
Be allowed to take Troy by
Himself. There's glory

For us all! Someone
Tell Agamemnon. Someone
Tell Menelaus.

PATROCLUS

Achilles will be
Always one step behind you.
Duck, parry, run, hide,

Turn around. There will
Be Achilles' sword pointed
At your breast. Kill him!

HECTOR

I will not be cowed
Though ghosts taunt me, gods forget
Their debt, I will fight.

The fight continues

ASTYNAX

Why do you hold me?
I would see my father and
Give him my support.

CHORUS OF TROJAN WOMEN

Look! He's badly hurt.

PRIAM

Which one? The years cloud my eyes
Though they fight close by

ASTYNAX

Daddy!

HECTOR

Astynax!

ACHILLES stabs HECTOR

HECTOR

Go below and do not watch.
Go away, boy. Now!

ACHILLES kills HECTOR

ANDROMACHE

Hector!

PRIAM

Take the boy!
Flee to your home! All of you!
To your homes! Go! Now!

Close the gates!

ODYSSEUS

Call the
Men to arms!

AJAX

To arms! To arms!
Signal to advance!

CHORUS OF SOLDIERS

We stand ready!

CHORUS OF TROJAN WOMEN

Run!
Soon they will cross the field and
Breach these very walls.

CHORUS OF SOLDIERS

Wake the camp! Sound the
Alarm. We follow.

ODYSSEUS

What's this?

AJAX

Achilles stirs not

Our prince attacks not.

CHORUS OF SOLDIERS

Why not? What is going on?
We're poised to attack!

ANDROMACHE

Oh, gods! Why? Why? Oh,
Cruel Achilles. What have I
Done for you to take

My whole family.
Father, brothers, lover and
Father to my son

ASTYNAX

Let me go, mother.
I will avenge my father
And kill Achilles

Though I am a child
Let me go to the city
Gates and meet my fate.

PRIAM

Achilles leaves. He's
Taking Hector's body to
The Greek encampment.

THERSITES

It's done. The yelling
Tells the tale.

BRISEIS

I must prepare
For his return. Soon.

THERSITES

Why would he come back?
Surely Troy is in turmoil.
We can take it now.

BRISEIS

Achilles did not
Come to Troy for Troy nor face
Hector for Hector.

He is coming soon.

> *ACHILLES drags HECTOR into the
> Greek camp*

ODYSSEUS

You bring the body here? Don't
You want to enter

The city and reap
The rewards of conquest?

AJAX

We're
Here to follow you.

> *ACHILLES leaves the camp and enters
> his tent*

BRISEIS

Welcome back, my lord.

PRIAM

Take him home, my girl.

> *ANDROMACHE leaves with
> ASTYNAX*
>
> *PRIAM is left alone on the stage*

PRIAM

I must
Go to Achilles.

> *He starts off*

INTERMISSION

SCENE 8
The Walls of Troy
The Outskirts of the Greek Camp
Later

ANDROMACHE is alone

ANDROMACHE

Love! Husband! The streets
Are so quiet and empty,
Husband! Do you hear?

The silence scares me!
You cannot leave me here. You
Cannot leave me here

To wait for that man
To come and to claim his prize,
Or to be sold to

Some nearby king to
Boost our dwindling ranks with fresh
Bodies for Greek spears.

Husband! Love! Someone
Wails for thee! It must not be.
The rumors of your

Death must not be…must
Not be. Come back and embrace
Your loving wife. Take

Me. Hold me in your
Arms and we can laugh away
The nightmare that has

Caught us and forces
Us to sleep, to dream, in dread,
Ever-constant fear

Of what horrors will
The morrow bring. What wives will
Stand on these walls and

Cry "farewell lost love!"
Love! Let me not be one of
Those sad sad widows.

Husband! Abandon
Not your wife and son to life's
Harsh realities.

Husband! Lover! Come
Back to me! Do not leave me
Like this! So alone!

Husband! Husband. Do
You hear? Are you listening?
Will you abandon

Us so? How dare you?
How dare you leave us for some
Pointless heroics?

I did not wed you
To be a widow, nor bear
Astynax to be

Another orphan,
To sit and watch other sons'
Fathers father sons.

Damn you! Not like this!
I could not bear it without
You, dearest husband.

Enter ASTYNAX

What is it, child? Why
Are you out of bed? The night
Is dark, full of woe.

ASTYNAX

It's my fault, mother.

ANDROMACHE

What, dear, is your fault? Hush, now.
Think not about it.

ASTYNAX

Father's death. Blame me!
The fall of great Hector, our
Hero, prince, our hope.

ANDROMACHE

No longer hope, child,
Nor Troy nor Hector longer.

ASTYNAX

Hope for vengeance—

ANDROMACHE

No!

No vengeance. No blood
Debt. Dead is dead. Do not hate
His killer. Fear him.

I would rather cast
You from these walls myself than
See you hunted by

Fell Achilles.

ASTYNAX

But
I distracted him. Killed him.
In vengeance I should

Strike myself down. Throw
Myself from these walls. Instead,
I will face the man

Who held the sword I
Guided.

ANDROMACHE

Do not speak so. He
Wanted you to flee

This city of death.
Would that he had fled too and
Lived a coward. Lived.

ASTYNAX

Father would never
Have hidden from Achilles
Or any other.

My father was no
Coward.

ANDROMACHE

Heroes die sooner
Than cowards. They leave

Their loved ones. Now, we
Are alone. No father. No
Love. No one to keep

The cold at bay, or
Fend for us against the beasts
That lurk just beyond

The glow of Troy's light.
Two legs or four, they circle
And wait for us to

Fall so they can feed
On the carcasses of our
City and our dead.

Better a coward,
Boy. Live and love your mother,
Not be food for beasts.

*The CHORUS OF SOLDIERS is
revealed in their camp*

CHORUS OF SOLDIERS

I'm hungry. Cannot
We cook something to eat? Why
Are no fires allowed?

Will some flickering
Fleck of fire fuel Achilles'
Wrath? So what, then. Don't

We want…nay…we need
Our fell princeling to smash the
Gates and let us in.

They say the streets are
Made of marble and the signs
Engraved with silver.

I've heard that the lights
Are so bright you can't even
See the stars at night.

Who needs such a light?
What depravities are they
Up to that they must

Blind the gods, who then
Cannot see, nor know, nor judge?
It boggles the mind.

Boggles? Boggles. I
Would prefer debauchery
In the dark. No doubt

Your women would, too.
P'raps in the dark your ears will
Trick you. Perhaps their

Snores will sound like sighs.
They say the Trojan women
Bathe every day.

They soak their bodies
In water while we thirst here
By the shores. Water!

Fresh water! Women!
Food! Jewels! The city is
Filled with treasures ripe!

Tempting! Tasty! Gods!
Why can't we storm those creaky
Gates? Achilles lolls

About his tent as
We shiver in the morning
Chill, our winter capes

Worn thin over the
Years. He feasts among the first.
Drink we capture flows

Up ere it flows down
Our throats. Now, Patroclus is
Dead, p'raps Achilles

Now flows. How soon will
He tire of Briseis and
Send her out to us?

How soon will he tire
Of unresponsive Hector?
And come out for us?

More wine! Where's the wine?
In Thersites gut. No, on
Achilles' tent's floor.

'Twas an ill-conceived
Maneuver. It saved us. But
For how long? What is

Going on in that tent?
Do I even want to know?
Who has the better

Fate: the dead Hector
Or live Briseis? Don't think
About such things. Look

To Troy, gods-blinding
Troy. It is oddly dark, now.
They mourn lost Hector.

There can't be many
Men left in there any more.
Grandmother Priam

And a few weedy
Princes. More sheaths than spears stand
Watch on Troy's ramparts.

They wallow in soft
Beds with soft women. Too soft.
'Twould make me hard 'nough.

Then take your spear and
Ram your way through Trojan gate.
Would be easy to

Slip right in. The gates
Are wide and used to many
Men trafficking through.

Then what is keeping
Us? I'll charge those walls, scale them,
Slaughter the nothings

Left behind. Forward
For our glory. Not for kings'
Princes' and heroes'.

No. Onward. Forward.
Our war. Our victory. Our
Lives. Our blood. Our deaths.

Death. Yet another
Consideration. Nonsense.
Achilles has killed

Hector. None stand in
Our way. Forward for glory!
For women! For gold!

Wait! Stop! Someone stands
Upon the Trojan wall. Who
Could it be? Hide! Hide!

CHORUS OF TROJAN WOMEN
is on the wall

CHORUS OF TROJAN WOMEN
Do you see any
Men? I see no men. No men
On either side of

These great walls. What's the
Point in defending yourself
If no one tries to

Conquer? Throw down these
Damn walls. Let the beasts come. Let
Then seize us. Let them

Take us. I tire of
Watching men burn on ev'ry
Fired pyre. Let these Greeks

Come and get over
With it. I hear these savage
Men are as hairy

Without their garments
As with. Ah, me!

ANDROMACHE
(Overlapping)

Ah me! What shall pass
With us? Me? My son?

CHORUS OF TROJAN WOMEN

What shall become of
Us? Will I be taken by
A great prince? I swear

Ajax saw me the
Other day. He winked at me.
Ajax? That blind fool.

He sees a woman
But is just as likely to
Spear a sheep. Although

I hear he has a
Mighty spear. If you're a sheep.
Now, Odysseus.

There's a man. Squat and
Bowlegged. Then what about
Menelaus. Right!

No man cuckolded
By the likes of Paris could
Satisfy a real

Woman. If he came
To me I would simply wave
Him along. Wave him

Along. I'd almost
Prefer Paris. Yes, you would.
What's that supposed to

Mean? Just that I saw
You over to the palace
The other day. There

You were, batting your
Eyelashes and laughing at
Everything that

Little toad said. I
Never! Did, too! Did not! Did
Too! Did not! Quiet!

CHORUS OF SOLDIERS

What was that noise? Did
Someone see us? Who goes there?
There! I see no one.

But there are shadows
There on those great heights. There are
Still giants in Troy

To leap 'cross the plains
And slay simple souls like us.
Fierce they are. Angry.

Filled with wrath over
The death of their hero. The
death of great Hector.

CHORUS OF TROJAN WOMEN

It is so boring.
So, so boring. Their campfires
Roar somewhere out there

Or is that the sea
That chants and marches in the
Night, beyond the camps,

And keeps us awake,
Expecting it to march 'cross
The plain and beat down

Our gates and to flow
Through our streets, washing away
All Troy, all of us?

Do they wait, out there?
Wait for us?

ANDROMACHE

Wait for me, love.

CHORUS OF SOLDIERS

All this waiting. We

Wait while our princes
And kings enjoy the pleasures
Of war. We die while

They enjoy all the
Treasures of war.

ANDROMACHE

Am I to
Spend my years waiting

To join you? Waiting
For our son to age and charge
Out and fight and die

And leave his widow?
Should I wait to see his sons
Orphaned? Left alone?

Enter AJAX and ODYSSEUS

AJAX

What is all this, then?

ODYSSEUS

Are they planning mutiny?

AJAX

I think that they are.

CHORUS OF SOLDIERS

No, no. Great princes.
We stand guard bravely over
The walls. Eyes on Troy.

AJAX

You are nowhere near
The walls.

CHORUS OF SOLDIERS

There are archers there.
Can you not see them?

AJAX and ODYSSEUS duck

ODYSSEUS

Did you lure us here
Hoping we would be pricked by
Trojan arrows?

CHORUS OF SOLDIERS

No!

AJAX

The walls are too far.
No arrow could reach us here.

ODYSSEUS

See who's on the wall.

AJAX

I will.

ODYSSEUS

Well?

AJAX

What?

ODYSSEUS

Look!

AJAX

Where?

ODYSSEUS

At the wall.

AJAX

It's a wall.

ODYSSEUS

Who's standing on it?

AJAX

No one. The men sit
Here. Next to the fire. With us.

ODYSSEUS

Not our wall. That wall!

AJAX

Ah. The Trojan wall.

ODYSSEUS

Yes! On the Trojan wall.

AJAX

Why
Would our men be there?

Would be dangerous.

CHORUS OF SOLDIERS

With Achilles. I'd feel safe
With fell Achilles.

On the wall, of course,
Not in his tent, I wouldn't.

ODYSSEUS

Shut up!

CHORUS OF SOLDIERS

What?

ODYSSEUS

Shut! Up!

Look, Ajax. Cast your
Eagle eyes across the dark
And blood-stain'd fields that

Lead to fair but ill-
Fated Ilium and tell
Us what heroes wait

Upon her ramparts.

                    AJAX

Huh?

                    ODYSSEUS

What?

                    AJAX

What?

                    ODYSSEUS

Well?

                    AJAX

Did you say?
Again.

                    ODYSSEUS

Again?

                    AJAX

Yes.

                    ODYSSEUS

Fine. Ajax. Cast your
Eagle eyes across the dark
And blood-stain'd fields that

Lead to fair but ill
Fated Ilium and tell
Us what heroes wait

Upon her ramparts.

AJAX

What?

ODYSSEUS

Gods! Ajax! Look. Over.
There.

AJAX

There?

ODYSSEUS

There! And tell.

Me. Me! Who stands on
The walls of Troy

AJAX

Oh! You want
Me to look over

There and tell you who
Is up there.

CHORUS OF SOLDIERS

I think he's got
It. Took long enough.

ODYSSEUS

Yes! 'Eagle eye.' We
Should call this one 'bird brain.'

AJAX

I
Heard that!

ODYSSEUS

Wasn't me.

AJAX

Whoever it was.
I've got my eye on you, so,
Watch out! Let me look.

CHORUS OF TROJAN WOMEN

What can you see? Naught
Save the gloom of approaching
Death. A Prophetess

You are now? You and
That royal pain, Cassandra.
She has had it rough.

Each prophesy wrong.
Absolutely wrong. Well, she
Did say that bringing

Helen into the
City would lead to war. Of
Course. But you did not

Need a seer to
Figure that one out. She did
Say Hector would fall.

Again, you hardly
Need divine gifts to know that.
Now, she's made the king

Get rid of all the
Horses. How will a horse bring
About the fall of

Troy? What will the Greeks
Do, hide under one? Perhaps
They'll hide inside one?

You could not fit more
Than one or two inside a
Horse. Unless it was

A very big horse.
It would have to be really
Big. Even then, you

Could fit only so
Many inside. It would be
Quite smelly and dark

In there. Of course, they
Are Greeks and would be used to
That. So how would they

Get inside? They're Greeks.
They know how to stick their heads
Up a horse's ass.

And when they'd come out
Covered in blood and sweat and
Filth, they'd be ready.

And so would we! Oh,
Will that tiresome woman stop
Crying over her

Dead husband?

ODYSSEUS

What do
You see along the field of
Battle? What is there?

AJAX

A haze spreads across
The way. It hides them from the
Sight of mere mortals.

ODYSSEUS

A haze?

AJAX

A haze.

ODYSSEUS

There
Is no haze. The sky is clear.
The night stars are bright,

Almost within reach.
Even I can see shadows
On the walls.

AJAX

You say

Your sight is better
Than mine.

ODYSSEUS

I say that I can
See shadows up there.

Can you not?

AJAX

Perhaps
The gods will not let me see.

ODYSSEUS

Perhaps you are blind.

AJAX

I am eagle eyed.
My keen sight stuff of legends.

ODYSSEUS

I can see the walls.

You would most likely
Walk into one.

AJAX

Take that back.

ODYSSEUS

Myopic Ajax.

AJAX

Damn you!

ODYSSEUS

That explains
His penchant for white-hair whores
Who bleat.

AJAX

What mean you?

ODYSSEUS

Baa!

AJAX

Take that back!

ODYSSEUS

Baa!

AJAX

That is it! You have sneered your
Last, Odysseus

The fox. Clever man.
Have at you!

ODYSSEUS

You can't even
See me.

AJAX

Well enough.

The CHORUS OF SOLDIERS cheers

ANDROMACHE

Do those men, those beasts,
Laugh and cheer the death of my
Husband? What kind of

Men applaud the death
Of any man, base, noble.
They are beasts. My son,

Do not listen. Do
Not. Cover your ears.

ASTYNAX

Ears that
Burn with anger, in

Disgrace at the sound.
Oh, father, do you deserve
Such ignominy?

Does your spirit hear
The mockery? Do you burn
With shame, e'en in death?

ANDROMACHE

Hush, child.

ASTYNAX

No, mother.
I do not hush. I'm no child.
I take my father's

Place. I will not give
Way and forget. Vengeance is
A father's son's right,

His obligation.
I would not dishonor him.

ANDROMACHE

You? Dishonor him?

You would dishonor
Your mother, only just a
Widow, to take her

Son from her. Would you?
Listen, my son, my flesh, my
Hector's flesh and blood.

Your father fought so
That you could live. His spirit
Craves comfort through your

Life. So many have
Gone ahead. They will serve him
In death. Serve him in

Life.

CHORUS OF TROJAN WOMEN

Leave her alone.
She'll mope for days. I am tired
Of all this mourning.

The Greeks, I am told,
Have no culture they have not
Stolen, no native

Philosophy. Their
Rough hands, rough caresses would
Be such a relief.

I can hardly wait
Until this foolish war, which
We must lose, ends. Look!

There goes King Priam.
Duck down so he won't see.

ANDROMACHE

There
Is the king. Leave him

To his own grief. He
Has no need to be burdened
By our loss.

CHORUS OF TROJAN WOMEN

There goes

The waddling old fool
Priam, begging for money.
Beggin our money.

What a coin purse is
He. More an accountant than
King. Will he take more

Of our gold? Just to
Ransom Hector's carcass? Are
The bodies of our

Husbands so paid for?
Is Hector's body worth more?
Is it? Speak, widow!

Shh! Not so loud. What's
That?

Cheering comes from the Greek camp

They are ready to come.
Best have more wine, first.

It's a bit chilly.
Best to get inside. Let the
Men wait on the wall.

*The   CHORUS   OF   TROJAN
WOMEN leaves*

AJAX

Ouch!

ODYSSEUS

That really hurt!

AJAX

I'm bleeding!

ODYSSEUS

I think I broke
My wrist. My fingers.

AJAX

I'm bleeding! Bastard!

ODYSSEUS

Leave me alone!

AJAX

My nose! My
Beautiful nose! Oh!

ODYSSEUS

I want to go home!

AJAX

Ha!

ODYSSEUS

What do you mean by that?

AJAX

You're an idiot.

You'd probably get
Lost on the way.

ODYSSEUS

Take that back.

AJAX

Make me!

ODYSSEUS

I'll pull off

That nose of yours

AJAX

Ow!
Let…You son of a—

ODYSSEUS

Ouch! Not
There! Let it go! Oh!

AJAX

Help! Help! He bit me!

ODYSSEUS

I did not.

AJAX

There's no biting.
That's how women fight!

                         ODYSSEUS

Are you calling me
A woman?

                           AJAX

You and Hector's
Corpse!

                         ODYSSEUS

Oh, my. That's just

Really so hurtful.

                           AJAX

Yeah? Well…you…deserved it.

                         ODYSSEUS

It's
Just so mean!

                           AJAX

Well. I….

                         ODYSSEUS

And to say I'll not
Get home. I mean, how stupid
Do you think I am?

                           AJAX

No. Not stupid. Not….
C'mon, Odysseus. Look.
Look. I didn't mean….

                         ODYSSEUS

Everyone says that
I'm pretty smart. That's my thing,
You know. And to say—

AJAX

I'm sorry. Really!

CHORUS OF SOLDIERS

Someone is coming.

AJAX

Where?

ODYSSEUS

Who?

CHORUS OF SOLDIERS

The lights are gone on

The wall.

AJAX

They're up to
Something.

ODYSSEUS

They're sneaky bastards.

AJAX

What if?

ODYSSEUS

What?

AJAX

They have....

CHORUS OF SOLDIERS

What!?!?

AJAX

Special arrows that could
Reach us.

ODYSSEUS

The bastards.

AJAX

Hide!

CHORUS OF SOLDIERS

Get down here! Off
My hand!

ODYSSEUS

Get your foot out of....
I trust that's your foot.

AJAX

Yes. That. Is. My. Foot.

CHORUS OF SOLDIERS

Quiet! No one will find us
Here! Someone's coming.

ODYSSEUS

I'm sorry about
Your nose

AJAX

Me, too.

ODYSSEUS

You've been a
Good friend. A true friend.

AJAX

'Twas a beautiful
Nose.

ODYSSEUS

Yes, it was. It still is.

AJAX

Do you think so? Truth?

ODYSSEUS

It's the finest nose
I have ever known.

AJAX

Friend?

ODYSSEUS

Friend.
We shall never fight.

AJAX

Never fight again.
Odysseus!

ODYSSEUS

Ajax!

CHORUS OF SOLDIERS

They
Do this ev'ry day!

But soft. I hear a
Step approaching. A soft tread
That turns alert ear

Towards mourning Troy.
But the faintest whisper, the
Slightest noise.

AJAX

What?

ODYSSEUS

Huh?

CHORUS OF SOLDIERS

Someone's coming from
Over there.

ODYSSEUS

Hide!

AJAX

Wait! Until
They pass.

ODYSSEUS

Then attack!

ANDROMACHE is alone on the stage

ANDROMACHE

Night is dark, Hector.
Fires have been doused in both camps.
There's no light tonight.

The moon herself hides
In shame behind curtains of
Cloud. Your light is snuffed.

The sun will not rise
Again to glimmer and glint
Off your golden mail.

No light. No heat, love.
There is no warmth in Hades'
Embrace. Hide, moon! Hide!

Hector's light will warm
You no more. Sun. Stay beneath
The waves. Your fiery

Beams and bright rays will
Not pierce the void. Ever night
Remains. Troy is dead.

Husband! My lover!
Your city's lights failed this night.
The putrid dark will

Engulf it yet. No
Hope. The shadows will devour
Both song and laughter.

Night is rushing in,
Like a great wave. It is building
Up and hanging like

A great swell, poised to
Wash away all in its path.
Even the brightest

Walls cannot withstand
It. I will wait, my husband.
I will await the

Dark. Perhaps when it
Has flowed past, left my rotting
Body in its wake,

I will find you. Find
You in Hades. P'raps you will
Remember me then,

And hand in hand, heart
To heart we will face whate'er
The dark gods do will.

Goodnight, my Hector.
Friend. Husband. Heart's light. Night's warmth.
Dearest love, goodnight.

SCENE 9
Achille's Tent - Later

> *ACHILLES is busy abusing Hector's body*
>
> *HECTOR (the ghost), BRISEIS, and THERSITES (still a ghost) are present*

                         BRISEIS

Are you sure he'll come?

                         HECTOR

He will come.

                         THERSITES

Someone's coming.
Feel it in the air.

                         HECTOR

I can't.

                         THERSITES

You will. Soon.

                         BRISEIS

Priam isn't so stupid
To put himself in

Achilles' angry

                         THERSITES

Hands. Wrath burns combat's fiery
Fury. Hector's dead.

HECTOR

It happened quickly,
But hurt more than I had feared.

THERSITES

My death was painless.

HECTOR

Your neck was snapped. No
Time for pain. I gave a quick
Death to Patroclus.

BRISEIS

You didn't hate him.
Patroclus was no one to
Hector but a foe

To be struck down, killed,
Forgotten like the others.
You learned how to kill.

But hatred was not
A lesson taught in Priam's
Troy, a city of

Light and peace. Hatred
Will be learned by those of us
Who survive this war,

The wives, the children,
They, we, will learn the hatred
That burns in men's hearts.

We will continue
The war for generations
Until all are dead.

All. Greeks and Trojans.
When, finally, no one is
Left who can sing of

Bold deeds of heroes
Or listen, with movéd hearts,
To violent deaths

Then, and only then,
Will this war be over.

                                    HECTOR

That
Will never happen.

There will always be
A Greek or a Trojan heart
Beating in some land.

Perhaps the Trojan
Children will flee this place and
Thrive in another

But they'll remember
They'll hide. They will bide their time
Until they're ready.

Then they will strike. They'll
Swarm 'cross Greek lands and leave your
People with nothing.

                                    THERSITES

Our heroes will fight.
They won't permit conquest by
The Trojan backwash.

                                    HECTOR

Your heroes will die.
Our heroes will die. In the
End, men will decide

The fates of the great
Cities, peoples, cultures. What
Heroes will be left

To Fight? With Hector's
Death, so goes Achilles, and
The others follow.

Heroes will breed men—
Dim, shadowy reflections
Of what was once great.

I felt something.

THERSITES

Yes.
It is now time. He has come.

HECTOR

My father is here.

PRIAM enters

PRIAM

You are Achilles?
It has been years since I've been
In a battle tent.

Years that have seen my
Children born grow and, yes, seen
Many of them die.

Years that have seen my
City grow and become a
Great power in the

Empire. It held its
Head high in the great courts. Men
Feared, respected it.

Now she lies, prone and
Vulnerable to your base
And violent lust.

The years have not much
Changed the inside of a tent
Made for warriors.

Pretty much the same
Trophies, I see. Even a
Beautiful young slave—

She amuses you
I trust. Armor of the dead.
And their spirits, too.

Funny thing about
War. About battle. About
The dead left behind.

You know why I'm here.
What now would you have me do
To deserve my son?

Should I fall to my
Knees? Would you have me kiss th'hands
That took my son's life

And left me alone
Undefended in a world
That grows colder, more

Dangerous each day?
Would you embrace the man who
Left your father so?

Would you? Could you? Would
Your father? I know him. I
Suspect he would not.

Nor will I. I will
Not kneel. I will not embrace
You. I can respect,

But there's no love in
My heart for you. You are a
Killer. Killer.

I may have my faults,
Yet I also have my pride.
I am a king. I

Was a father. Yes,
To be sure, I have sons left.
But what are they next

To Hector? Nothing.
They are callow. They're selfish
Weak, vain, and stupid.

I do love them, in
My way. What father cannot?
But there was Hector.

A golden child, a
Golden warrior, general
Of our hearts and minds.

To Hector I gave
All of my hopes and my dreams.
He was the reason

For my past; he was
The future of my people.
He was a bright light

That allowed us to
Awaken and face a day
Darkened by Greek clouds.

I—I can see him:
Young, imperious, bullying
His slaves and playmates;

Returning home from
His first hunt, the taste of fresh
Blood upon his lips;

Taking a woman,
Still reeking of the flesh of
A freshly killed foe.

I can still smell the
Terror of his wedding night,
The stench of young love.

I have so many
Memories that live in my
Senses—gentle touch,

A giggle, a sigh;
The taste of sweat on his face;
The brilliance of his

Smile; the aroma
Of battle. Hector was a
Good son. A great man.

My other sons pale
Next to him. I will not meet
His like again. No.

What memory will
Be strongest, will always burst
In my mind's eye, will

Be that of watching
My son fight with you and then
Watching you kill him.

I understand why
You hated him, had to kill
Him. He killed you heart,

And you have killed mine.
I hate you. I would kill you
If I could, fight you

If I dared. I can't.
I daren't. I am too old,
Too feeble for it

There is but one thing
I can do. I can beg. You'll
Not survive this war.

This I know. You know.
The fiercest flame burns all in
Its path, then flames out.

The gods have shown me
Your death, the weeping slave girls,
Your allies confused

And stunned, rejoicing
Trojans. But the gods have not
Shown me who kills you.

P'raps it's a Trojan
Out of self preservation.
Or, perhaps, a Greek

Jealous of glory
Or booty; or maybe shamed
By your attention.

What would you have done?
What should we do when you're dead?
And your bloody and

Broken body lies
In an enemy's tent, to
Be so abused far

From home, far from love,
Far from your father's tears, far
From your mother's love?

What would you have done?
Would you have your body left
As food for vultures?

Or would you be sent
To your father, so he could
Bid his son farewell,

So he could embrace
You, bathe your face in the tears
Of his grief? What would

Your prefer? Oh, great
Achilles, conqueror, please
Give me back my son!

Let me honor him;
Let his wife and mother clean
His body; let his

Son weep over him;
Let his people show respect
To their dead hero.

Give me back my son!
I beg you this! I beg as
Much as pride allows!

Let hatred flow from
You. You've venged Patroclus. Oh,
Give me back my son.

You are Achilles
"The Conqueror." Be "The Just"
Give me back my son.

Keep your slave women.
Keep your hostages. Keep the
Treasures that I've brought—

Treasures that beggar
My people, my city, me.
Give me back my son!

Noble Achilles,
Son of divine Thetis, please
Give me back my son.

PATROCLUS

Passionate is your
Father, Hector.

THERSITES

But a fool
To trust Achilles.

He'll certainly die.
Achilles—

HECTOR

He trusts not the
Man. He trusts the son.

PATROCLUS

I trust the lover.

HECTOR

Who has gotten his vengeance.

THERSITES

What else, then, is there?

HECTOR

There is Patroclus.
My women cleansed him, cared for,
Prepared his body.

So Patroclus can
Go to the gods an honored
Corpse, not one abused

> ODYSSEUS *and* AJAX *burst into the tent*

ODYSSEUS

Please give him his dead.

AJAX

Then Priam can join his son
Helped by a sword thrust.

HECTOR

No doubt there are men
Without to help them kill an
Old man here alone.

AJAX

Speak, old man, before
We kill you. Who let you in
Past vigilant guards?

PRIAM

This is my home! I
Laid every stone. I ploughed
Ev'ry field. I have

No need of a guide.
I am king here. Unhand me.

BRISEIS

He is a guest here.

PATROCLUS

Hospitality
Is not a virtue among
Greeks.

HECTOR

Are there any?

THERSITES

This is fun.

BRISEIS

This is
Infamous! Have you no shame.
A defenseless man!

ODYSSEUS

He could have come with
Heralds and horns under a
Flag of truce. Perhaps

Agamemnon would
Have honored him. Perhaps not.

BRISEIS

Your king is a beast!

AJAX

My king is a king!

BRISEIS

So is Priam!

AJAX

Quiet, whore!

PRIAM

Quiet, Briseis!

AJAX

Listen to your king.

PRIAM

I came to speak with the man
Who killed my Hector.

Are you he?

AJAX

No.

ODYSSEUS

No.

PRIAM

I will speak with Achilles.
I'll have none of you.

AJAX

You'll have—

ODYSSEUS

None of us?

THERSITES

What delightful arrogance.

ODYSSEUS

I am not a child

To be so dismissed.

AJAX

I should rend you limb from limb.

ODYSSEUS

I'll cut off your head.

Come, Ajax, bring him.

PRIAM

You'll do nothing of the sort.
I am an old man,

Yes. I'm no coward.

ODYSSEUS

You've spent this war behind walls.

PRIAM

You have spent this war

Behind Achilles.

ODYSSEUS

I will not tolerate such

Insolence from you!

PRIAM

I came to this camp,
Which pollutes my shores, to see
Achilles, not you.

ODYSSEUS

Yet here we are.

AJAX

Yes.
And you must face us, fool.

PRIAM

You
Will find me ready.

AJAX

You have no weapons.
He has no weapons. The breeze
From my mighty swing

Will blow him to the
Ground. When I have entered Troy
I'll toss your grandson,

Hector's royal brat,
From the walls like offal.

HECTOR

He
Will do no such thing.

THERSITES

He will. He's a beast,
Remember? Animals do
As animals do.

There is no point in
Being angry with them.

HECTOR

A
Mad dog is put down.

ODYSSEUS

Be careful, Ajax.
He's a wily man; he must
Be up to something.

AJAX

Some cunning Trojan
Trick, is it? Think to trick me
Old man? Is that it?

PRIAM

Unhand me! I will
Gouge your eyes out.

HECTOR

Let him go!

THERSITES

Let them have their fun.

PATROCLUS

There's no profit in
This.

ODYSSEUS

There's no profit in this

AJAX

Profit?

ODYSSEUS

Profit.

AJAX

Gold

ODYSSEUS

Hold him for ransom.

AJAX

What an idea.

ODYSSEUS

I'm glad
I had it.

PATROCLUS

Are you.

ODYSSEUS

Yes. We hold him. We
Demand the Trojans give us
Gold for his return

AJAX

We'll be rich.

HECTOR

You'll be
Dead before you're paid.

THERSITES

Oh, please!
What are you thinking?

PRIAM

My people won't pay.

ODYSSEUS

Then Ajax can have his sport

BRISEIS

You will send him home.

ODYSSEUS

We will send him home—
Piecemeal.

AJAX

Yes, piecemeal. Ha!

ODYSSEUS

You

Don't know what that means.

AJAX

There are people here.

ODYSSEUS

Sorry.

PRIAM

Get your hands off me.

AJAX

I'll gut you old man!

ACHILLES

Priam's in my tent.
He is mine to kill or not.
Ajax, stand you down.

I swear, one day you'll
Die, and it will be my sword
That opens your gut.

Do you think that the
Father of my greatest foe
Could get to this tent

Without my knowing
He was coming? Ajax, you
Underestimate

Me. Odysseus,
You overestimate your
Own intellect if

You think I cannot
See your paw-prints all over
The pain of this night.

If any killings
More are to be done today,
Let them be by me.

How many deaths are
On your head since this nightfall?
How many tears shed

Because of you and
Ajax? Odysseus, you're
Clever without thought.

You sent Patroclus,
A man past his prime, out to
Fight our enemy's

Greatest hero. With
Whom did you think we were at
War? A gathering

Of callow boys and
Doddering philosophers?
Priam's old, but he

Had the courage to
Stand up to you just now; I
Suspect he might have

Gouged out your eyes ere
You had managed to killed him.
Could you face Hector?

By the time Hector
Met me on the field, he had
Already lost. He

Was already dead—
So great was his fear. So great
Was his father's fear.

He faced me, though. He
Stood before me, raised up his
Shield and swung his sword.

You could not even
Approach me to tell me of
Patroclus' death. What

Sort of man are you?
You send this drunken fool, a
Target, to my wrath.

To be sure, I killed
Thersites, and I would have
Most likely killed you.

You'd have died a man.
Hack down whom you will in the
Heat of battle; that

Is a man's fortune.
Priam came to see me in
Proud humility.

He is sacrosanct.
At least for the moment, at
Least while I'm alive.

War is glorious!
Battle is grand! The heat warms
The blood and the heart.

Killing should be hot.
It should be blind. Cold, sighted
Killing is murder.

I'll have none of that.
I do not care who wins or
Who loses this war.

You. Build your cities.
You. Tear them down, burn them down.
Rise or fall. Live. Die.

I am a killer.
Some, like Hector, fight to save
Their people, their ways

Of life. Troy may be
A great city. It may shine
In the annals of

History for years,
Centuries, millennia.
One day it will fall.

If not to the Greeks
At least the ravages of
Time must bring it down.

Your bold temples, the
Towers that reach to the clouds
And challenge your gods

Will be, must be, one
Day but ruins in a vast
Wasted desertland.

Slabs of rock, piles of
Dried mortar, bones and rusted
Weapons. What will those

Who find your city
Know of Troy? What will they say
Of your people then?

Perhaps they will make
You gods. Your petty struggle
Make Olympian.

Perhaps our gods are
But failed heroes, dead soldiers,
Withered prostitutes

Whose bones lie bleached by
Eons of pounding sun on
Some forgotten field,

Stained by years of dirt,
Or in a distant tomb, or
Crushed into mortar.

And they spy on us
From our walls and our ceilings.
There's god! In the door,

Underfoot! In the
Piss pot! If I blaspheme, god
May splash on my shoes.

Odysseus, you
And Ajax have sat with me
In council. You speak

Of gold and in the
Same breath long for glory and
Immortality.

Pray tell me, what good
Is immortality? What
Good is glory? Will

You live forever
To enjoy great epic poems
Sung by weaklings and

Fools so blinded by
Hero worship they'll ne'er know
The reasons we fight?

Do you really care?
You will be dead. You won't watch
Your descendants. You

Can't hear your women
Lamenting when they light your
Bier. It's folly to

Worry. You die. That's
It. Your gods will not care if
Your flesh cooks or rots.

The maggots might care.
The birds. The fish. Perhaps your
Spirits might linger,

Afraid of the void
That reaches for them, knowing
Nothing lies beyond,

Convinced that if they
Can tell their stories to the
Living, it will change

Their fates. Their fates, your
Fates, My fate. We will die. Where's
The mystery there?

Where is the glory?
Where is the poetry and
The heroism.

Hector died so that
Troy could stand. It must fall, if
Not now, then someday.

Odysseus will
Live and die for songs he won't
Hear or understand.

I kill because I
Enjoy it. I like to take
Life, to see the eyes

With comprehension
Dull in despair. Yes, I thrill
To the fight, the kill.

I am most alive
Especially when I,
Achilles, am close

To death. Today I
Destroyed a work of art. The
Finest warrior

Of his age. I took
His life from him, from his son,
His wife, his father.

I've satisfaction
In being the hero of
The age. Kings come to

Beg favors from me.
Women belong to me. Men
Long to be with me.

I take what I want.
I go where I want. I'm who
Others want to be.

Someday I'll parry
Too slowly, raise my shield when
I should lower it

Duck too late. Someone
Else will don the mantle of
Hero, birds will pick

Out my eyes and worms
Eat my flesh. Putrid smell will
Be my legacy.

The opinions of
Allies and enemies mean
Little to me, dead

Or alive. Love me,
Hate me, as you will, but fear
Me. I insist on't.

Priam is a brave
Man. P'raps the bravest here for
He expects to die.

He knows, he fears, that
At any moment I might
Reach out and snap his

Fragile neck and toss
His carcass out as offal.
Yet, he has come here

Not withstanding. He
Has shown me respect. On the
Other hand, you have

Come here angrily
Making demands, convinced that
I am your tame pet,

A trained lion that
Nibbles sweetmeats from the hands
Of your pretty queens—

Who sit not quite so
Alone in your dingy forts
Waiting your return—

Rather than that king
Of cats, the tiger, waiting
To tear the hand off,

Rip away the flesh
And maul the quivering mass
That's left of the corpse.

You both insult me.
Your men waiting to rush in
Is further insult.

Priam can take his
Son home and give him proper
Rites in respect to

Whatever gods he
Chooses. He may take his son
Unmolested from

This camp. Whatever
Man or fool dares hinder him
Will answer to me.

Priam, I killed your
Son. I'm not sorry for that,
But for your pain, yes.

Hector offended
Me. That is why I killed him;
I'd do it again.

I'd still regret your
Pain. In another life I'd
Be honored to serve

A king such as you.
Better than these gossiping
Timid old women.

Go Priam. Go now.
They won't harm you. They will not
Dare it, even though

Ambushing grieving
Old men and corpses is what
They excel at. Go!

Take your ransom. I'll
Not live long enough to spend
It. Do not kneel at

My feet. Rather, take
My hand. Take my hand. Go! I
Vouch for your safety.

You there! You! Come in!

The CHORUS OF SOLDIERS enters

ACHILLES

Bear Hector's corpse back to Troy.
Carry him with pride.

Bear him rev'rently.
He died a better man than
You, though you live. Take

Him up. And guide his
Father, respectfully, home.
Do not abuse him.

Do not mock his pain.
Do not leer at his women.
Take them, then return

Bearing Patroclus.
We trade body for body,
Love for love. All right?

In a week you can
Continue slaught'ring Trojans.
Until then, you rest.

They leave with PRIAM

ACHILLES

Odysseus. You
And Ajax can return to
Your tents. When they come

Back with Patroclus,
I will hold games in honor
Of him. His spirit

May rest thereafter.
You two will stay in your tents
Until the games are

Over. If I see
Either of you during that
Time, I'll kill you both.

Get out.

ODYSSEUS and AJAX scurry off

ACHILLES

Briseis
Wait for me in the other
Room. I'll be in soon.

She leaves

ACHILLES

There are too many
Ghosts here. Too many damn fools.
Why do you remain?

Are you so afraid
That you will be forgotten?
Thersites. No one

Knew who you were while
You lived. No one cared. Take some
Comfort there. No one

Thought enough of you
Even to hate you. Now you
Will be remembered.

Hector, a brave man
Risked all for love of you. He's
More like Achilles

Than the others are.
You faced death for your city.
You faced death for Troy.

What is Troy? What does
It mean? Is it all that much
More than a rock pile.

Towers, buildings, homes,
Temples waiting to be ruins?
Is it really more

Than a collection
Of people waiting to die?
Where's the glory there?

Where's the glory in
Stasis? Does certain death bring
Immortality?

Did you die for your
Family? If so, why not
Spend the years with them?

Now you can but haunt
Them, hoping to hear your name
Praised, sacrificed to,

Extolled. What sort of
Life, future, have you given
To them? Your son now

Walks in the footsteps
Of a hero, a martyr.
Can he measure up?

Should he avenge your
Death? Should he strive, he toil for
Immortality

As well? Can he hope
To compare? What life is that?
What future has he?

Will he ever be
Anything but Hector's son?
Your wife must now sleep

Alone. Who would dare
Take a god's place in her bed?
She'll wither and die

Alone, abandoned.
No one can succeed Priam.
He may have other

Sons, but who of them
Is not callow and weak? Who
Can save your city?

Your death was an act
Of selfishness, Hector, a
Study in hubris.

Now you come to haunt
Me, Patroclus. What were you
Thinking? What kind of

Fool were you to face
The youth of Troy, the might of
Hector on your own?

Was my mail enough
To stop a sword, my blade to
Slice through iron and shield?

Was Patroclus so
Great a warrior? I am
Not shielded by gods

Or distant magics.
Even I, Achilles, bled
Ere I slew your bane.

As a man, you were
Lovely and tender and kind.
Was it not enough

For you—my love, my
Heart and my youth? Why did you
Leave me? For glory?

Did you honor me?
Did you care so much for this
Pitiful war? Can

You ever begin
To answer that? No! Don't speak!
So many shining

Lives! Why did your spark
Have to be snuffed? Even the
Most gilded life can

Not shine without light!
I can hate Hector, but I
Can't blame him for it.

You. You. You. You doused
Your light foolishly and took
It away from me.

You took away the
Illumination. You took
Away your light's warmth.

Where's the love in a
Cold and clammy corpse? Can it
Smile to greet the morn?

Can it laugh like a
Babe or cry like a woman?
Do you embrace it?

Can you love the dead
Or do they simply linger
Hov'ring out of reach?

No touch. No caress.
No more gazing at stars or
List'ning to the sea.

No more drunken nights
Of debauchery, no more
Women, no more men.

I'd have killed for you,
Conquered kingdoms, crossed seas, braved
Vast deserts for you.

Now, all I can do
Is mourn. Your foolish pointless
Death is all that's left.

Even your mem'ry,
Like your spirit, must soon fade.
Already you dim.

You, Hector, even
Vile Thersites were bright lights
That eclipsed the sun

With your lives and fear
Hopes and loves and your passions.
Now your flames falter

And soon...so soon...your
Flames will be dimmer, colder
Than the distant stars.

You could have lived for
Years burning fiercely. Now you
Fizzle and dwindle.

There's no meaning in
Death, no glory, no honor.
There's nothing but death.

And by your deaths you've
Left me with nothing. Nothing!
What should I live for?

Whom should I burn for?
Who is there now to love for
And fight and die for?

Who will thrill to my
Conquests? Sew my wounds? Who will
Hold me when I fail?

You have abandoned,
Left me without audience
Left me without flame.

Do I care what they,
Men non-men like Ajax or
Odysseus, think

Not-think? They are fools.
Do I care what a brave king
Like Priam thinks? What

Will he tell children
Around the hearth? He is the
Enemy. It is

Enough that he fears.
Hector? It is enough that
He dies. Nothing more.

You were my glory.
You were my audience. You.
You have taken that

From me. Think of it.
What have you left me with? There
Is no more warmth left

There is no more light.
All that remains is darkness
For me to swell in.

I don't like the dark.
Cold, no love, no lovers, no.
Reach out to nothing.

Reach out my fingers
And try to grasp onto the
Blackening darkness.

Just out of reach. There's
Always something, just past the
Horizon, past touch.

I lie in my black
Pit and listen to whispers
Just beyond hearing.

I roll over on
The bed and feel the empty
Spot just abandoned.

No longer warm, but
Not yet cold. A taunt, a tease
Just to remind me.

Who will bring light to
My tent? Who will keep it warm?
Who will wait for me?

Begone, ghosts! Haunt me
No more! Do not think that I
Cannot kill you yet.

Patroclus, how could
You leave me? You were all the
Glory I needed.

Hector, how could you
Not win? You would have saved Troy.
You'd be immortal.

Begone, ghosts! Begone!
Go to whatever heaven
Or hell that you know.

Victory or loss.
I don't know which is the worse.
Dead, alive—alone.

Loss. Death. Nothingness.
Absolute as a void, no
Dreams, yet no nightmares,

Nor no pain nor joy
Nor hope nor love nor hate nor
Other emotions.

P'raps victory's worse.
The ruled will never love the
Rulers. The dead can't

Love their killers. The
Women are never honored.
Slaves can't be trusted.

Their friends resent them.
Their allies fear them. Those they
Saved, those they bled for,

Those they and their sons
Strove for, suffered for, and died
For will then hate them.

The victor looks o'er
His shoulder not for fear of
His enemies. No—

Enemies can be
Seen, anticipated—but
For fear of his friends.

No doubt many of
These Greek kinglings will find their
Homecomings far more

Perilous than the
Bloody Trojan battlefields.
Far more dangerous

Than the roughest sea's
Tempests. At least the dead don't
Live long enough to

Know how feeble and
Brief is the flame of fame and
Immortality.

The victors live to
Become paranoid, see their
Statures diminish,

Watch themselves die a
Little every day. What fate
Waits for Achilles?

When can I die and
No longer fear a life lived
Alone? Answer that!

I don't want to be
The ever hero; I just
Want to be the man.

Now, though, what purpose
Would it serve? Patroclus is
Gone. A long life warmed

By a steady glow
No longer has its appeal.
Let me then flare up,

Eclipse the distant
Stars, burn more brightly than the
Sun, devour all the

Other light around,
Build and grow until all men
Are blinded by the

Fury of my flame,
Are seared by my heart, and then
Let me be snuffed out.

Let my light end; let
A shadow cover the sky
And make my world dark.

Spirits, ghosts, begone!
Death is a cold place, but you'll
Find no more warmth here.

The fires have been doused.
Lanterns turned down. The moon has
Ridden to her home,

And her brother the
Sun rises. It is feeble
And will not warm us.

The living must feel
The chill; so must the dead. So
Ghosts, spirits, begone.

HECTOR and THERSITES leave

ACHILLES

Where does the sun's fire
Come from? Fiery steeds driven
By a distant god?

Perhaps the great fire
Comes from our hearts when we lose
Someone whom we love.

Or perhaps it is
Simply a burning rock that
Circles 'round this Earth.

Someday it will run
Out of fuel, sputter, die, and
Then winter will reign.

Go to the sun. See
If it can warm the dead and
Then wait for me there.

As surely as sun
And moon rise and set I will
Be joining you soon.

PATROCLUS leaves

ACHILLES

I will spend my last
Days on fire. Women will cry
In lamentation.

Men will die by the
Score. Cities will fall. Many
Heroes will rue these

Coming weeks. I'll give
Poets reason to sing of
Me, remember me.

Achilles may die.
Though his flame be snuffed, it will
Heat generations.

ACHILLES leaves

CURTAIN

About the Author

Edward Eaton has studied and taught at many schools in the States, China, Israel, Oman, and France. He holds a PhD in Theatre History and Literature and has worked extensively as a theatre director and fight choreographer. As a writer, he has been a newspaper columnist, a theatre critic, and has published and presented many scholarly papers.

He is the author of the young adult fantasy time travel series *Rosi's Doors*, which includes <u>Rosi's Castle</u>, <u>Rosi's Company</u>., and <u>Rosi's Time</u>. He is also the author of the dramas <u>Elizabeth Bathory</u>, <u>Hector and Achilles</u>, and <u>Orpheus and Eurydice</u>.

In addition to his academic and creative pursuits, Ted is an avid SCUBA diver and skier. He currently lives and works in Boston, Massachusetts, with his wife Silviya, a hospital administrator, and his son Christopher.

www.ingramcontent.com/pod-product-compliance
Lightning Source LLC
Chambersburg PA
CBHW051824040426
42447CB00006B/349